A *Hometown* CHRISTMAS

We wish you a Merry Christmas

A
Hometown
CHRISTMAS

IDEALS PUBLICATIONS, A DIVISION OF GUIDEPOSTS
NASHVILLE, TENNESSEE
WWW.IDEALSPUBLICATIONS.COM

ISBN 0-8249-4125-X

Published by Ideals Publications, a division of Guideposts
535 Metroplex Drive, Suite 250
Nashville, TN 37211

Library of Congress Cataloging-in-Publication Data
A hometown Christmas
    p. cm.
    ISBN 0-8249-4125-X (alk. paper)
    1. Christmas—Literary collections. 2. American literature. I. Ideals Publications Inc.
    PS509.C56 H66 2000
    810.8'0334—dc21   00-046090

Printed and bound in the USA by RR Donnelley & Sons, Willard, Ohio.
Color Film Separations by Precision Color Graphics, Franklin, Wisconsin.

10 8 6 4 2 1 3 5 7 9

Publisher, Patricia A. Pingry   Copy Editor, Elizabeth Kea
Book Editor, Julie K. Hogan   Editorial Assistant, Amy Johnson
Art Director, Eve DeGrie   Research Assistant, Mary P. Dunn

Spot Illustrations by Gail Roth

ACKNOWLEDGMENTS

ALDRICH, BESS STREETER. "Journey into Christmas" from *Journey into Christmas and Other Stories*. Copyright © 1949, 1963 by Meredith Publishing Company, renewed. Used by permission of Dutton, a division of Penguin Putnam Inc. BOWEN, ELIZABETH. An excerpt from "Home for Christmas." Copyright © 1955 by the Conde Nast Publications, Inc. All rights reserved. Reprinted by permission. CLAPP, LUCRETIA D. "The Fir Tree Cousins." Published in *Christmas in My Heart 3*, Review and Herald Publishing Association, Copyright © 1994. Text used by permission of Review and Herald Publishing Association, Hagerstown, MD 21740, and Joe Wheeler, P.O. Box 1246, Conifer, CO 80433. CROWELL, GRACE NOLL. "Leisure" and "Let Us Keep Christmas." Used by permission of the author's estate. ENGEL, DAVE. "Home Church Christmas." Used by permission of the author. FARJEON, ELEANOR. "The Children's Carol" from *Poems for Children*. Copyright © 1927, 1955 by Eleanor Farjeon. Reprinted by permission of Harold Ober Associates Incorporated. FISHER, AILEEN. "Merry Christmas" from *Feathered Ones and Furry* by Aileen Fisher. Copyright © 1971, 1999 by Aileen Fisher. Used by permission of Marian Reiner for the author. FYLEMAN, ROSE. "Christmas-Time." Reprinted by permission of The Society of Authors as the Literary Representative of the Rose Fyleman Estate. GRIGSON, JANE. Excerpt from "In Dulci Jubilo: A Table for Carolers" by Jane Grigson from *Christmas Memories with Recipes* edited by Maron L. Waxman. Copyright © 1988 by Jane Grigson. Copyright © 1988 by Book-of-the-Month Club, Inc. Reprinted by permission of Farrar, Straus and Giroux, LLC. GUEST, EDGAR A. "Homecoming." Used by permission of the author's estate. HOLMES, FRED L. "An Orange in Our Stockings" from *Side Roads*. Copyright © State Historical Society of Wisconsin. HOLMES, MARJORIE. "Give It to Somebody Who Needs It" and "Sing a Song of Christmas Carols" from *At Christmas the Heart Goes Home*. Copyright © 1991 by Marjorie Holmes. Reprinted with permission of the

author. LAWRENCE, D.H. An excerpt from *The Rainbow*. Copyright © 1915 by D.H. Lawrence, renewed 1943 by Frieda Lawrence Ravagli. Used by permission of Viking Penguin, a division of Penguin Putnam Inc. McCORD, DAVID. "Come Christmas" from *All Day Long*. Copyright © 1965, 1966 by David McCord. By permission of Little, Brown and Company (Inc.). McDONALD, JULIE. "The Lesser Christmas Miracle." Reprinted by permission of the author. MILNE, A.A. "A Hint for Next Christmas" from *If I May* by A.A. Milne. Copyright © 1921 by E.P. Dutton & Co., Inc., renewed 1949 by A.A. Milne. Used by permission of Dutton, a division of Penguin Putnam Inc. NASH, OGDEN. "Nutcracker Suite Narrative" from *The New Nutcracker Suite and Other Innocent Verses*. Copyright © 1962 by Ogden Nash, renewed. Reprinted by permission of Curtis Brown, Ltd. SANSOM, CLIVE. "Snowflakes" from *An English Year*. Reprinted with permission of David Higham Associates Limited. SPENCE, HARTZELL. "Christmas in the Parsonage." Used by permission of the author. TORME, MEL and WELLS, ROBERT. "The Christmas Song (Chestnuts Roasting On an Open Fire)." Copyright © 1946 by Edwin H. Morris & Company. A Division of MPL Communications, Inc. Reprinted with permission of Hal Leonard Corporation. TRUITT, GLORIA. "The Loving Gift." Reprinted by permission of the author. VAUGHN, BILL. "Tell Me a Story of Christmas." Reprinted by permission of The Kansas City Star. WORTH, VALERIE. "Christmas Ornaments." Reprinted by permission of George Bahlke. Our sincere thanks to the following authors whom we were unable to locate: Herbert Asquith for "Skating"; Shirley Bachelder for "Angel on a Doorstep"; Anne Campbell for "The Old-Fashioned Sleigh Ride"; X.J. Kennedy for "Christmas Chime"; Alison Uttley for "Waiting for Christmas." All possible care has been taken to fully acknowledge the ownership and use of every selection in this book. If any mistakes or omissions have occurred, they will be corrected in subsequent editions, provided notification is sent to the publisher.

PHOTO CREDITS

Cover, pp6–7 © Linda Nelson Stocks p11 © FPG, CAT#T7-5172; p13 © Jessie Walker, 00069-01975.0043; p15 © FPG, CAT#16865; p20 © FPG, CAT#T7-3492; p23 © FPG, CAT#21122; p27 © SuperStock, 164/2865G/B/E13; pp28–29 © Linda Nelson Stocks; p35 © FPG, P17600; p36 © FPG, CAT#25279; p39 © FPG, SF#014154; p43 © SuperStock, 2016/537160/I/H2D; p44 © FPG, CAT#13188; p47 © FPG, SF#014174; p49 © Nancy Matthews, 1712B; pp52–53 © Linda Nelson Stocks; p58 © FPG, BB18719; p61 © FPG, SF#007599; p62 © Johnson's Photography, 23019-00307; p69 © SuperStock, 155F/838C/B/H2G; p73 © FPG, CAT#21122; pp74–75 © Johnson's Photography, 23019-00703; p82 © H. Armstrong Roberts, KX-11459; p85 © FPG, X51326; p86 © H. Armstrong Roberts, KX-11981; p91 © Johnson's Pho-

tography, 22077-00902; pp94–95 © Linda Nelson Stocks; p100 © SuperStock, 1031/169/I/R57G; p102 © Johnson's Photography, 22019-00107; p107 © FPG, SF#016239; p109 © Daniel Dempster, 16064; p110 © H. Armstrong Roberts, KW-13729-j; pp114–115 © Linda Nelson Stocks; p121 © Daniel Dempster, 16065; p124 © H. Armstrong Roberts, KX-13008-j; p126 © FPG, CAT#13181; p129 © Johnson's Photography, 23019-00613; p135 © H. Armstrong Roberts, KX-13034-j; pp136–137 © Linda Nelson Stocks; p141 © SuperStock, 538/126642/O/C2; p143 © Johnson's Photography, 23091-00809; p145 © Jessie Walker, 00036-01125.0053; p147 © Jessie Walker, 036-2373-156; p154 © Johnson's Photography, 43077-00412; p156 © The Crosiers, 464065; p159 © H. Armstrong Roberts, KX10956

Contents

Christmas
WISHES
AND
DREAMS

We Wish You a Merry Christmas

Traditional

1. We wish you a merry Christmas, we wish you a merry Christmas, we wish you a merry Christmas and a happy New Year. Good tidings to you, wherever you
2. Oh, bring us some figgy pudding; oh, bring us some figgy pudding; oh, bring us some figgy pudding, and a cup of good cheer.
3. We won't go until we get some; we won't go until we get some; we won't go until we get some, so bring some out here.

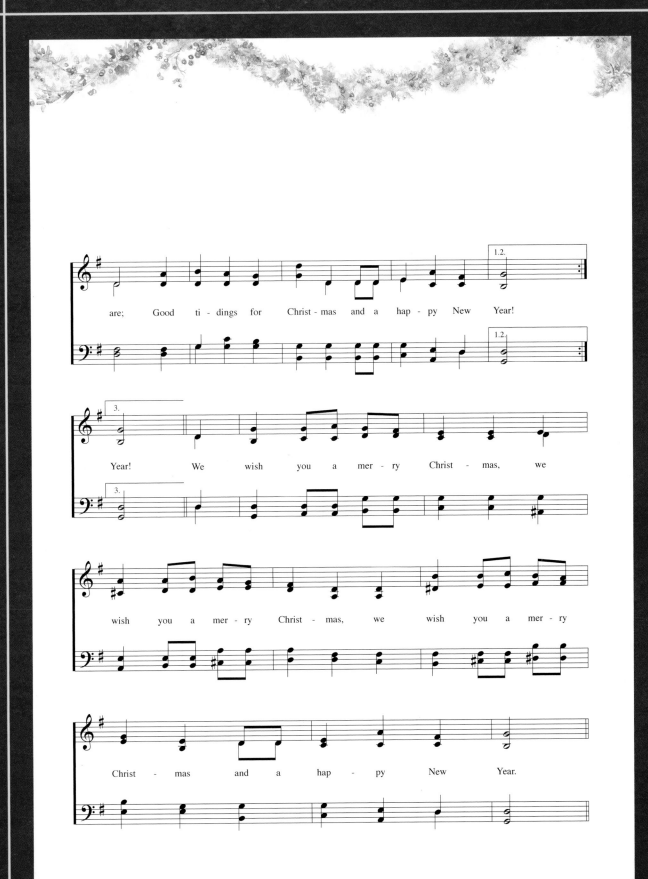

Sing a Song of Christmas Carols

MARJORIE HOLMES

*You merry folk, be of good cheer,
For Christmas comes but once a year.*
—GEOFFREY SMIGH

*D*eck the Halls With Boughs of Holly . . . And wash the curtains and polish the silver. And clean out the fireplace and haul in the wood . . . And try to find the old tree base. And dig out those cartons of decorations to see how many are good for another year.

While Shepherds Watched Their Flocks by Night . . . Sit up late making doll clothes. And finishing a sweater and painting a sled. And helping your husband uncrate a bicycle . . . And then steal around checking on your own flock before collapsing into bed.

Good Christian Men, Rejoice . . . When the last box is finally wrapped and tied and in the mail, and you're at least halfway through addressing the greeting cards.

We Three Kings of Orient Are . . . Bearing gifts we traverse afar: to church and parties and school bazaars. And shut-ins and hospitals and children's homes. And that family whose mother is ill and whose father is out of a job.

0 Come, All Ye Faithful . . . joyful and triumphant that somehow it's all done! The church bells are ringing, it's time to come . . . Come, children and neighbors and aunts and uncles and cousins—come and behold Him. O come, let us adore Him!

Away in a Manger . . . No crib for a bed—a three-year-old is curled up in a pew, fast asleep.

It Came Upon the Midnight Clear . . . That little voice calling out: "Is it morning yet? Did Santa Claus come?"

Silent Night, Holy Night . . . All is calm, all is bright . . . at last . . . It is, it truly is . . . Sleep in heavenly peace.

Hark! the Herald Angels Sing . . . At the crack of dawn, "Get up, get up, Merry Christmas!"

Joy to the World . . . Let earth receive her king . . . And people their gifts, and parents their hugs . . . Let children run back and forth to each other's houses, and

neighbors pop in for a cup of wassail and to admire the shining tree . . . Let heaven and nature and your own heart sing!

God Rest You Merry, Gentlemen . . . And women. Let nothing you dismay! Even though the whole house is an explosion of candy, nuts, papers, presents, and ribbon; the tags are so mixed up nobody knows who to thank for what; and the cat is knocking the ornaments off the tree.

Add another log to the fire snapping so fragrant on the grate, baste the turkey already golden in the oven. Fling open the door to grandparents and other guests who come tramping up the snowy walk. With true love and brotherhood, each other now embrace.

God rest you merry, mothers and fathers and families and friends, at the end of this glorious Christmas day!

A Festival of Lights

KATHERINE BUXBAUM

Christmas is the shining festival of the unselfish.
It is the homecoming of the spirit, the glorification
of all that is good. —AUTHOR UNKNOWN

The two great festivals of the Christian year have been so cherished by Moravians that a whole fabric of traditional practices peculiar to the sect has been woven around these seasons. In matters like these we did not mind at all being "different," but gladly laid hold of the inheritance that was ours.

Christmas in the Lapham neighborhood really began with the baking of the cookies. Early in December people began speaking for the cooky cutters. A clever tin-smith back in Ohio had made a specialty of turning them out in fancy shapes, birds, stars, Christmas trees, and a dozen different animal shapes, including a reindeer, whose outlines were the despair of amateur cooky bakers and the triumph of those expert ones who could turn out crisp, thin reindeer with all their horns intact. House-wives borrowed freely and cheerfully lent the cutters; non-Moravian families made the cookies, too; and when the cutters passed on to the next baker they were always accompanied by a sample of the batch. We grew to be connoisseurs of cookies; Mrs. Niedermeier's were the thinnest—a great distinction—but were almost too "brickle." Mrs. Thaeler's were just right; she spared neither shortening nor spice, and balanced amounts of molasses and sugar to a nicety. Since the recipe was in terms of quarts and pounds, no wonder the yield was prodigious. A peck measure full of shapes was a commonplace in the household.

There was another mystery with which a few of the initiated were busy during December. The making of candles for the Christmas Eve service was the special prerogative of the oldest women in the congregation, the pioneer mothers who had made candies for home use long before lamps were common. They took great pride in their product, a perfect candle made in the molds they had brought with them to the West. How patiently they coaxed the string that was the wick down through the small hole in the end of the mold, and what pains they took to get the candies out clean and whole and shapely. Then each one must be trimmed with a little petticoat of frilled paper, to catch the wax that would run down the side when the candle was

lighted. I speak of what I later learned to know of the process. As children we saw only the finished product, and although we had it each year it was always a new and beautiful surprise.

Adults might pretend that all this fuss over cookies and candies was for the children; as a matter of fact, they were expressing themselves in these creative enterprises. It was the same with decorating the church, only this time it was the younger people who claimed their prerogative. Let the old folks and the children stay out of this, especially the children. They were not to see the decorations until the supreme moment of Christmas Eve itself.

On the afternoon of the twenty-third the young men would meet at the cemetery to cut the green that would be needed and bring them up to the church lawn. This was an exciting event, as pines were rare in our section, and besides there is something festive about the very smell of evergreen in December. Returning from school that afternoon I felt my heart leap at the sight of the jolly pile outside the church, and I longed for the day when I would be one of the important people who should take a hand in the decorating.

When the young men came back in the evening the girls would be there too. Their cheeks glowed with the cold when they unwound their "fascinators." Toes and fingers tingling, they stood around the stove chatting for awhile; then someone would say, "Well, I suppose it will be festoons again." Of course it would be festoons. The Sunday before, a committee had been appointed to arrange for decorating, but the basic plan always included ropes of evergreens at the windows and spanning the chandeliers. While the boys brought in the boughs the girls hunted up the carpet warp saved from former years. Then they sat down, two by two and began the business of festoon making. Who sat with whom was very important; and the newest romantic attachment was made public in this way. There was something magnetic about the occasion, as there was about the season itself. Winter brought leisure, for one thing; the relentless drive of farm work slowed up, and people felt relaxed, less matter-of-fact than usual. Christmas was an appropriate time for lovers' avowals. Young men might speak their minds on Christmas Eve, when hearts were tender, and when music and poetry (like that in the Bible) charged with allusions to childhood and the ties of home, made a common meeting ground for thoughts.

It would be almost midnight when they finished. They swept up the scraps of green and stepped back to admire the work of their hands. Now the familiar room seemed altogether transformed. The chill of its Puritan simplicity was softened by this gracious greenness, for festoons had been supplemented by wreaths in each window, and at the front of the room was an evergreen arch under which they had placed the minister's cherished Putz, a replica of the Nativity scene, complete with manger, cattle, and approaching Wise men.

Now on Christmas Eve the children came into their own. The "exercises" were theirs, and they were the usual thing: much singing and much speaking, solos or in concert. The mistakes were theirs too: a letter in the Merry Christmas legend held upside down; a verse spoken out of turn; too quick or too tardy an entrance into a dialog, if anything so advanced as a dialog was a program feature. People liked that sort of thing, but the costuming was the despair of those who coached the children. How, for instance, could a little girl who wore red flannels be appropriately dressed as an angel? We had no dressing room, and even if we had had one, it would have been risking health to make all the changes a thin summer dress would require! To dress boys as shepherds was another problem. In later years bath robes solved that one. The program committee felt reasonably sure that the Orientals wore bath robes or something very similar.

In all our entertainment there was no mention of Santa Claus. And the Christmas tree, if we had one, was just the tree itself, a symbol, as its inspired chooser, St. Boniface or someone else lost to legend, intended it to be. I am glad that our service did not include the practice of public gift giving. One heard of jealousies, heart burnings, rivalries, and boastings in those places where the Joneses sought to outdo their neighbors by putting a larger doll on the tree for their Mary than the Smiths could provide for their daughter. We were all treated alike with gifts from a common fund, and the gifts were only candy, an orange (rare, then) and the precious candle. This last was treated with appropriate symbolism. There is a Moravian hymn dedicated to the ceremony of candle passing, the one known as Morning Star, beginning: "Morning Star, O'cheering sight, Ere thou cam'st how dark earth's night."

The opening lines of each stanza are sung as a solo, then repeated by a quartet with the parts in harmony. Our ministers were particular to carry out this detail, and the assignment of the solo part was indeed an honor. Scarcely less of an honor was the privilege of passing the candles. As soon as the first strains of the hymn were heard, everybody watched to see who would come forward to carry the candle boards. It was usually a young married couple; better still an affianced pair. From behind a screen where someone had been busy lighting the tapers, they brought what looked like a tray load of blossoms, and children gave an ecstatic sigh at sight of all those wavering tiny flames. The couple started down the aisle, "he" carrying the board with a show of great caution, while "she" smiling, put the candles into outstretched hands, whispering something gracious, warning children not to get them too close to clothing or hair. All the while the Morning Star, which fortunately has many verses, had continued, and the last notes died away only when the last child in the room had received this coveted gift. After this the minister gave a brief talk about the Light of the World, while dreamy eyes looked into the flames, and heads turned so that eyes could see the room alive with candle glow. When we were told to put out our lights, carefully, one row at a time, there was much puffing, and much sniffing for the blended fragrance of wax and evergreen. Then while the smoke wisps faded on the air we rose for the last hymn, "Joy to the World," and for the benediction. For us it was the climax of the whole Christmas season.

The Scent of Christmas

Christmas Baking

Smiling, she rolled her dough with care,
Cutting the cookies one by one,
Some into stars and some to spare,
Shaping like Santas, just for fun.
Cinnamon, raisin, butter, spice,
Came from the oven warmly, sweetly.
What other smells could be so nice?
What other things so good to eat?

Filled to the brim, each cookie jar
Waited for Santa's yearly whim;
"Santa knows where the cookies are,
And leave some coffee just for him!

Maybe he'd like a midnight treat,
A chance to rock and doze a bit,
Then when he's had enough to eat
He'll start again on his happy trip.

Here, and perhaps in other lands,
Memory holds such cookie jars:
Mothers who rolled, with careful hands,
Spicy brown dough for Christmas stars,
Raisin-fat Santas, ginger trees,
Coconut angels to surprise
Happy Saint Nick, or just to please
Children who watched with shining eyes!

LOUISE WEIBERT SUTTON

Old-Fashioned Gingerbread with Lemon Glaze

1⅔	cups all-purpose flour		½	cup molasses
1¼	teaspoons baking soda		½	cup boiling water
1½	teaspoons ground ginger		½	cup vegetable oil
¾	teaspoon salt		⅔	cup powdered sugar
1	egg, lightly beaten		3	tablespoons fresh lemon juice
½	cup granulated sugar			

Preheat oven to 350° F. Grease and flour a 9-inch square baking pan; set aside. In a large mixing bowl, sift together flour, baking soda, ginger, and salt. Add egg, sugar, and molasses; mix well. Stir in boiling water and oil; mix until smooth. Pour batter into prepared pan. Bake 35 to 40 minutes or until top springs back when touched and edges have pulled away slightly from the sides of the pan. Place on a rack to cool. Sift powdered sugar into a small bowl. Stir in lemon juice, stirring until smooth. Drizzle glaze over the top of warm gingerbread. Cut into squares and serve warm or cold. Makes 36 bars.

Moravian Ginger Cookies

⅓	cup vegetable shortening, melted		½	teaspoon ground cloves
1	cup dark molasses		½	teaspoon ground ginger
½	cup packed dark brown sugar		½	teaspoon mace
1½	teaspoons baking soda dissolved in		1	teaspoon orange extract
2	tablespoons hot water		1	teaspoon salt
½	teaspoon ground cinnamon		4	cups all-purpose flour

In a large mixing bowl, combine melted shortening, molasses, brown sugar, and dissolved baking soda; mix well. Add cinnamon, cloves, ginger, mace, orange extract, and salt; mix well. Gradually add the flour. Wrap dough in plastic and refrigerate overnight.

Preheat oven to 350° F. Divide dough into four portions, taking out one-fourth and leaving the rest in the refrigerator. Roll out as thin as possible on a floured surface with plastic wrap on top of the dough. Cut out shapes with floured cookie cutters. Transfer to a parchment-covered cookie sheet. Bake 4 to 5 minutes. Remove cookies the instant they begin to lightly brown. Store in air-tight tins. Makes 8 dozen cookies.

The Fir Tree Cousins

LUCRETIA D. CLAPP

For somehow, not only at Christmas, but all the long year through, the joy that you give to others is the joy that comes back to you. —JOHN GREENLEAF WHITTIER

Mrs. Brewster sat in the middle of her bedroom floor, surrounded by a billowy mass of tissue paper, layers of cotton batting, bits of ribbon, tinsel, and tags. She was tying up packages of various shapes and sizes, placing each one when finished in a heaped-up pile at one side. Her face was flushed; wisps of cotton clung to her dress and hair, and she glanced up anxiously now and then at the little clock on the desk as it ticked off the minutes of the short December afternoon.

"I'll never be through, never!" she remarked disconsolately after one of these hurried glances. "And there's the box for cousin Henry's family that just must go tonight, and the home box. Oh, Nancy Wells . . ." She broke off suddenly as she caught sight of a slender little figure standing in the doorway, surveying her with merry brown eyes.

"Nancy Wells! Come right in here. You're as welcome as . . . as the day after Christmas!"

"So you've reached that stage, have you, Ann?" the visitor laughed as she picked her way carefully across the littered floor to an inviting wicker chair near the fire.

"Yes, I have. You know I always begin to feel that way just about this time, Nancy, only it seems to be a mite worse than usual this year."

Ann Brewster stretched out one cramped foot and groaned. "Here I am just slaving, while you, well, you look the very personification of elegant leisure. Well, you can just take off your coat and hat, Nancy, fold yourself up on the floor here, and help me out. I'm not nearly through, but I just must finish today. If there's one thing I'm particular about, Nancy, it is that a gift shall reach the recipient on time.

Nancy Wells looked about her appreciatively at the chintz-hung room glowing in the warmth of the open wood fire, and with its pleasant disarray of snowy paper and gay ribbons.

Ann paused and glanced at the clock. "My, look what time it is! I'll have to go.

I wonder if you'd just as soon stay, Nancy, and finish up that little pile over there by the couch. They're for the fir-tree cousins down on the farm."

"The fir tree cousins! Whatever do you mean, Ann?"

Ann laughed gaily as she stood up and shook off the bits of tinsel and ribbon from her skirt.

"Oh, I always call them that in fun," she explained. "They're Tom's cousins who live down in Maine. The idea struck me, I suppose, because theirs is the 'Country of the Pointed Firs,' you know. I've never seen any of them, but I've always sent them a box at Christmas ever since I've been married."

"What fun!" Nancy exclaimed enthusiastically. "How many are there, and what do you send them?"

"Let's see, there are Cousin Henry and Cousin Lucy, then the boys, Alec and Joe and little Henry, and one girl, Louise, who is just between the two older boys. And, oh, yes, there's Grandma Lewis, Cousin Lucy's mother." Ann ticked off the names on her fingers.

"Tom says they have a fine farm. He used to go there summers when he was a boy. I always buy their things long before any of the others. I hit upon a certain thing and stick to it as nearly as possible every year. It's easier."

"Why, Ann, you don't give them the very same thing year after year, I hope?" Nancy looked up in comical dismay.

"Well, why not?" Ann demanded a trifle sharply. "Take Cousin Henry, for instance. I usually get a nice warm muffler for him, because I'm sure he can . . ."

"But I should think . . ." Nancy interrupted. "My dear, it's just freezing cold there! They have terrible winters, and one needs mufflers, and more mufflers! You can't have too many. Then I nearly always pick out an apron of some kind for Cousin Lucy. One can't have too many aprons, either, especially when she does all her own work. For Grandma Lewis, I choose a bag or something to put her knitting in.

This year I found some sort of an affair for holding the yarn. I didn't understand it very well myself, although they told me it was perfectly simple; but I thought an experienced knitter like Grandma Lewis would know how to use it. Louise is just sixteen, so it's easy enough to select a pair of stockings or a handkerchief for her. As for the boys, Alec and Joe, I always get them neckties—they can't have too many, you know—and for little Henry a game or toy of some kind. Then Tom adds a box of candy. Promptly one week after Christmas I receive a perfectly proper, polite letter from Cousin Lucy, thanking me in behalf of every member of the fir tree household. It does sound a bit perfunctory, doesn't it, Nancy? Sort of a cut- and-dried performance all around. Somehow, Christmas is getting to be more and more like that every year; don't you think so? I must confess I'm glad, positively relieved, when it's over! I'm always a wreck, mentally as well as physically."

Nancy made no comment; instead she pointed with the scissors to a heap of large and small packages over at one side.

"What do you want done with those, Ann?"

"Oh, they go in the home box. That has to go tonight, too. I was just starting to tie them up. Do you suppose you'd have time to do them too, Nancy dear? Now I'm off. Good-bye, and thanks awfully."

A minute later Nancy Wells heard the front door slam, then the house settled down to an empty quiet, broken only by the rustling of tissue paper and the click of scissors as Nancy folded and cut and measured and snipped. The fire burned to a bed of dull embers; and beyond the small square windowpanes, the snow-lit landscape darkened to dusk.

"There!" said Nancy, as she gave a final pat to the last bow. "And how pretty they look too," she added, leaning back to survey her handiwork. Then she carried them over to the bed and arranged them in two neat piles.

"Certainly looks like 'Merry Christmas,' all right."

With which remark, she put on her coat and hat and went home.

It was several hours later that Ann Brewster surveyed with weariness, compounded with relief, the empty spaces on bed and floor. The last label had been pasted on while Tom stood by with hammer and nails, ready to perform the final offices. And the two boxes, the one for the fir tree cousins down on the Maine farm, the other for Ann's own family in Michigan, were now on their way.

"And now that's over for another year at least," she sighed. "And I'm too tired to care much whether those boxes reach their destination safely or not. Twelve months from tonight, in all probability, I shall be sitting in this same spot making that very same remark. And I used to just love Christmas too."

"Tired, Ann?"

A masculine voice broke in on her reverie, and Tom's broad-shouldered figure filled the doorway.

"Cheer up! The boxes are on their way, or should be shortly, and a few days more will see the season's finish."

"That's just it, Tom. We're losing the spirit of Christmas—the simplicity and good wishes, I mean, that used to be the big thing about it."

"You'd better get to bed now, Ann. You look tired to death."

The Thomas Brewsters faced each other across the breakfast table the morning after New Year's. There was a pile of letters beside Ann's plate.

"I know exactly what's in every one of these missives," she sighed.

Tom smiled as he opened his morning paper.

There was a silence for several minutes while Ann slowly slit the seals one by one. She picked up a square white envelope that bore her father's well-known handwriting, and a minute later a sudden exclamation made Tom look up.

Ann's eyes glanced down the single page; then she began to read aloud:

My dear Ann:

Perhaps you won't remember it, but you gave me a muffler for Christmas once long ago, when you were a very little girl. You picked it out yourself, and I'll say this, you showed remarkable good taste. That muffler, or what's left of it, is tucked away somewhere in the attic now. The one you sent this year gives me almost as much pleasure as did that other one, although I suppose I'll have to concede that these new styles are really prettier (but not any warmer or more useful) than the old. Your mother thinks they must be coming back into favor again, but I don't care whether they are or not. They're warm and they help keep a clean collar clean. For my part, I'm glad we're getting away from the showy Christmases of the last few years and down to a simpler, saner giving and receiving.

Lots of love and thanks to you and Tom.
Father.

Ann drew forth a small folded sheet that had been tucked inside the other one. It read:

Dear Ann,

I'm just going to add a line to put in with your father's, for we have a houseful of company and there's no time for a real letter. Your box this year, although something of a surprise, was nonetheless welcome. I have thought for several years that we ought all of us to give simpler gifts. A remembrance, no matter how small, if carefully and thoughtfully chosen to meet the need or desire of the recipient, carries with it more of the real Christmas spirit than the costliest gift or one chosen at random. I don't know when I've had an apron given me before! I began to think they had gone out of fashion. I put yours right on, and your father said it made him think of when you children were little. The boys will write you themselves, but I'll just say that Ned and Harold both remarked that they were glad you sent them neckties. (You know we've always tried to think up something different, with the result that both are rather low on that article.) We've had lots of fun with Hugh's game. He confided to me that he'd been hoping somebody would give him one. So you see, Ann, dear, we are all pleased with our things and send you our grateful thanks.

Love to you both from
Mother.

P.S. I was afraid my letter telling of your Aunt Cordelia's arrival had not reached you in time, but I need not have worried. She was much taken with that case for holding her yarn. She'd had one and lost it. And Katy was real pleased with that pretty handkerchief.

With a hand that trembled a little, and with burning cheeks, Ann drew forth the last letter in the pile. It was postmarked Maine, and contained two plain lined sheets, tablet-size. "This is from Cousin Lucy," Ann began, a queer little note creeping into her voice:

My dear Ann:

When we opened your box on Christmas morning, I thought I had never seen anything so attractive. Seals and ribbons and greetings may not mean so much, perhaps, to you city people; but for us isolated ones, they add a great deal to our enjoyment and appreciation. Your gifts fulfilled certain long-felt desires, one or two of which I suspect are older than you are, Ann. Perhaps you cannot understand the joy of receiving something you've always wanted yet did not really need. I am writing with my beautiful pin before me on the table. You see, it is the first one—the first really nice pin— I've ever owned. That is fulfilled desire number one. The second is the sight of your Cousin Henry enjoying a bit of leisure before the fire with his new book. I suppose Tom may have told you that once, as a young man, your Cousin Henry made this very trip to the headwaters of the Peace River. So few new, and worthwhile books find their way to us. Louise and the boys will write later, so I'll only say that Alec actually takes his big flashlight to bed with him; Joe is inordinately proud of that safety razor; and as for little Henry—well, his father and I both feel that we ought to thank you on our own behalf, for all our efforts to make an out-of-'door lad of him seem to have failed hitherto. He is the student of the family, but the new skates lure him outside and help to strike the proper balance. Louise loves her beaded bag, as, indeed, what girl wouldn't? And as for Grandma Lewis, she fairly flaunts that bit of rose point. She confided to me that at eighty years she had at last given up all hope of ever possessing a piece of real lace!

I have written a long letter, but I doubt if, after all, I've succeeded in expressing even a small part of our appreciation to you and Tom for your carefully chosen gifts. To feel that a certain thing has been chosen especially for you, to fit your own individuality and particular desire, if not always need—this, it has always seemed to me, is the true spirit of Christmas. Before closing I want to ask if you and Tom can't arrange to make us a visit this summer?

Wishing you both a Happy New Year,
Lovingly,
Cousin Lucy.

Ann Brewster laid down the letter with something that was half a sob and half a laugh. "I'm just too ashamed to live!"

"Why, what's the matter, Ann?" Tom looked puzzled.

"Cousin Lucy speaks of my 'carefully chosen gifts.' And they weren't at all. They weren't even meant for any of them. You see," Ann swallowed the lump in her throat, "I've always just chosen their things at random. Yes, I have, Tom. One of those Christmas obligations you spoke of the other night, to be disposed of with as little time and effort as possible. And then last week, when I was hurrying to get everything off, Nancy Wells came over and I left a lot of things for her to finish wrapping while I dashed off to the dressmaker's. And I suppose, in some way, I got the fir tree cousins' and the home pile mixed."

Tom pushed back his chair from the table.

"Seems to me, Ann dear, that we've had the answer to our query, 'What's wrong with Christmas?' You've sort of stumbled upon the truth this year, but—"

Tom stopped, whistling thoughtfully as he drew on his overcoat. There was a misty light in Ann's eyes as she stood beside him.

"When will you have your vacation, Tom?"

"August, probably."

"Well, we're going to spend it with our fir tree cousins! And, Tom, I can hardly wait!"

Christmas Wishes

Leisure

I shall attend to my little errands of love
    Early this year,
So that the brief days before Christmas may be
    Unhampered and clear
Of the fever of hurry. The breathless rushing
    That I have known in the past
Shall not possess me. I shall be calm in my soul
    And ready at last
For Christmas—the Mass of Christ—I shall kneel
    And call out his name;
I shall have leisure—I shall go out alone
    From my roof and my door;
I shall not miss the silver silence of stars
    As I have before;
And oh, perhaps, if I stand there very still
    And very long,
I shall hear what the clamor of living has kept from me—
    The angel's song.

GRACE NOLL CROWELL

O Holy Night

O holy night! the stars are brightly shining;
It is the night of the dear Saviour's birth.
Long lay the world in sin and error pining,
Till he appeared and the soul felt its worth.
A thrill of hope the weary world rejoices,
For yonder breaks a new and glorious morn;
Fall on your knees,
Oh, hear the angel voices!
O night divine, O night when Christ was born!
O night, O holy night, O night divine!

JOHN SULLIVAN DWIGHT

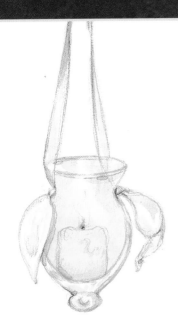

Kaleidoscope

Hold to your eye
The colors of Christmas:
Flame of poinsettia, holly's red,
Spicy greens, and the candles' glow;
Bright papers and ribbons,
A hundred cards,
And a cathedral's hushed, dim nave.

Hold to your ear
The sounds of the season:
Christmas carols from a dozen lands,
Joyous bells and their pealing,
Organ and choir and a child's high voice,
The silence of snowfall late at night.

Hold to your heart, oh, hold to your heart,
The unchanging dream of Christmas:
The shining Star that led Wisemen on
To a Babe in his mother's arms,
And, all about, the angels praying
As we must pray, as we all must pray,
"Peace on earth; good will to all men."

ELIZABETH SEARLE LAMB

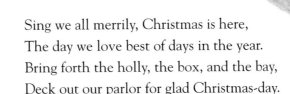

Sing we all merrily, Christmas is here,
The day we love best of days in the year.
Bring forth the holly, the box, and the bay,
Deck out our parlor for glad Christmas-day.

Sing we all merrily, draw round the fire,
Sister and brother, grandson and sire.
Sing we all merrily, Christmas is here,
The day that we love the best of days in the year.

AUTHOR UNKNOWN

Christmas Wishes

Wishing for you
All the special delights
Of this holiday season,
This season of lights.

Wishing the beauty
Of sparkling snow,
Of fir tree and holly
And gay mistletoe.

Wishing the joy,
The faith and the love
That God in His mercy
Sends down from above.

Wishing the love
Of the Christ Child dear—
The love that God sent
To His children here.

Wishing the peace
That knows only good—
The peace that unites us
In true brotherhood.

Wishing much joy
And happiness too—
May Christmas be blest
To your loved ones and you.

GERTRUDE ROSENKILD

Waiting for Christmas

ALISON UTTLEY

This is the night that love came down,
shedding its warmth on field and town.
—PAUL J. LIGHTLE

A few days before Christmas Mr. Garland and Dan took a bill-hook and knife and went into the woods to cut branches of scarlet-berried holly. They tied them together with ropes and dragged them down over the fields to the barn. Mr. Garland cut a bough of mistletoe from the ancient hollow hawthorn which leaned over the wall by the orchard, and thick clumps of dark-berried ivy from the walls.

Indoors, Mrs. Garland and Susan and Becky polished and rubbed and cleaned the furniture and brasses, so that everything glowed and glittered. They decorated every room, from the kitchen where every lustre jug had its sprig in its mouth, every brass candlestick had its chaplet, every copper saucepan and preserving-pan had its wreath of shining berries and leaves, through the hall, which was a bower of green, to the two parlours which were festooned and hung with holly and boughs of fir, and ivy berries dipped in red raddle, left over from sheep marking.

Holly decked every picture and ornament. Sprays hung over the bacon and twisted round the hams and herb bunches. The clock carried a crown on his head, and every dish-cover had a little sprig. Susan kept an eye on the lonely forgotten humble things, the jelly molds and colanders and nutmeg-graters, and made them happy with glossy leaves. Everything seemed to speak, to ask for its morsel of green-ery, and she tried to leave out nothing.

On Christmas Eve fires blazed in the kitchen and parlour and even in the bed-rooms. Becky ran from room to room with the red-hot salamander which she stuck between the bars to make a blaze, and Mrs. Garland took the copper warming-pan filled with glowing cinders from the kitchen fire and rubbed it between the sheets of all the beds. Susan had come down to her cosy tiny room with thick curtains at the window, and a fire in the big fireplace. Flames roared up the chimneys as Dan carried in the logs and Becky piled them on the blaze. The wind came back and tried to get in, howling at the key-holes, but all the shutters were cottered and the doors shut.

The horses and mares stood in the stables, warm and happy, with nodding heads. The cows slept in the cow-houses, the sheep in the open sheds. Only Rover stood at the door of his kennel, staring up at the sky, howling to the dog in the moon, and then he, too, turned and lay down in his straw.

In the middle of the kitchen ceiling, there hung the kissing-bunch, the best and brightest pieces of holly made in the shape of a large ball which dangled from the hook. Silver and gilt drops, crimson bells, blue glass trumpets, bright oranges, and red polished apples, peeped and glittered through the glossy leaves. Little flags of all nations, but chiefly Turkish for some unknown reason, stuck out like quills on a hedgehog. The lamp hung near, and every little berry, every leaf, every pretty ball and apple had a tiny yellow flame reflected in its heart.

Twisted candles hung down, yellow, red, and blue, unlighted but gay, and on either side was a string of paper lanterns.

Mrs. Garland climbed on a stool and nailed on the wall the Christmas texts, "God bless our Home," "God is Love," "Peace be on this House," "A Happy Christmas and a Bright New Year."

So the preparations were made. Susan hung up her stocking at the foot of the bed and fell asleep. But soon singing roused her and she sat, bewildered. Yes, it was the carol-singers.

Outside under the stars she could see the group of men and women, with lanterns throwing beams across the paths and on to the stable door. One man stood apart beating time, another played a fiddle and another had a flute. The rest sang in four parts the Christmas hymns, "While Shepherds Watched," "O Come, All Ye Faithful," and "Hark the Herald Angels Sing."

There was the Star, Susan could see it twinkling and bright in the dark boughs with their white frosted layers; and there was the stable. In a few hours it would be Christmas Day, the best day of all the year.

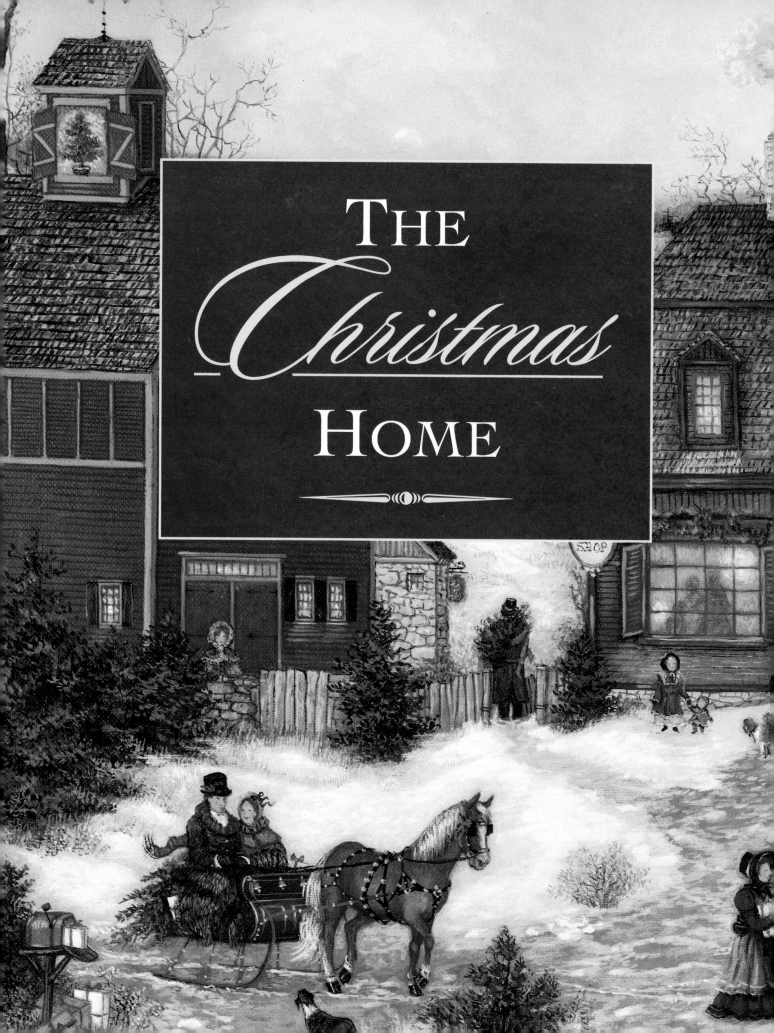

THE Christmas HOME

The Christmas Song

Mel Tormé and Robert Wells

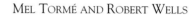

Chest - nuts roast-ing on an o-pen fire, Jack Frost nip-ping at your nose,

Yule - tide car-ols be-ing sung by a choir, and folks dressed up like Es-ki - mos. Ev-'ry-bod-y

knows a tur-key and some mis-tle-toe help to make the sea-son bright,

Ti - ny tots with their eyes all a-glow will find it hard to sleep to - night. They know that

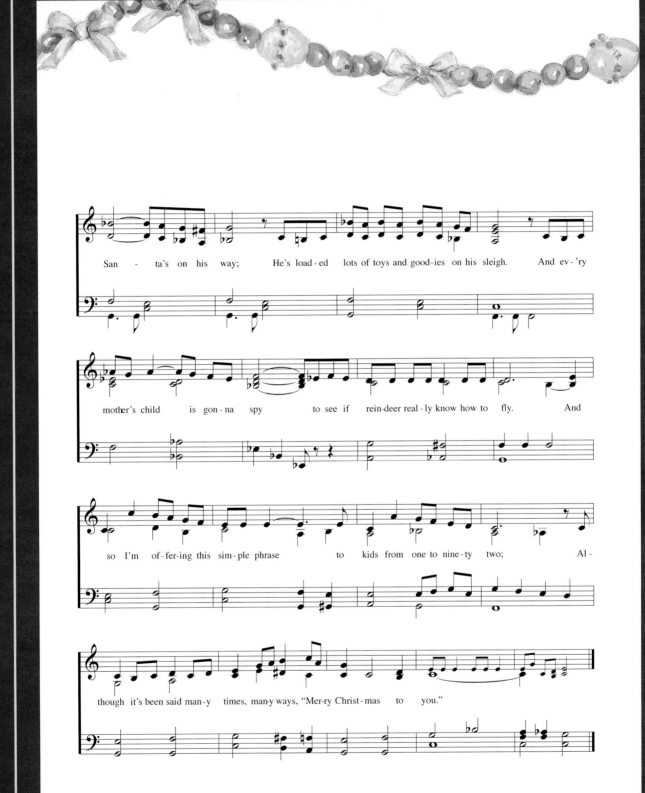

Home for Christmas

Home for Christmas

Away from the busy sights and sounds
I take the road toward home,
Back to the hills and the valleys,
Back where I loved to roam.

The snow is white and glistening,
The stars shine bright above;
I'm going home for Christmas,
Home to those I love.

The folks will be there waiting
With a smile and open arms;

I'll find warmth and laughter there,
The wealth of homey charms.

There'll be a Christmas tree in the window
As friends and neighbors gather 'round
To sing the songs of Christmas;
And joy shall there abound.

The road seems long and winding
But there's happiness at the end;
For I'm going home for Christmas,
And home is 'round the bend.

GLADYS BILLINGS BRATTON

It's a Great Night

It's snowing without, and the winds do howl;
How comfortable by the fire!
See how shadows are cast on the walls
As the flames rise higher and higher.

We'll talk of our friends and our blessings too,
And the beauties of true goodwill;
It's a great night for gathering 'round the fire
While the winds outside grow chill.

GEORGIA B. ADAMS

Homecoming

I watch them at the depot—
the mothers at the gate–
Who ask the age old question:
"Is the train on time or late?"
The annual tears of gladness;
the same sweet laughter gay;
The loved ones home returning
to spend the Christmas day.

I watch them staring, peering
along the railroad track
And think how glad the season
that brings the loved ones back!
How long and bleak the absence
of those obliged to roam!
But, oh, the joy of Christmas
which brings the children home!

Oh, glorious, happy moment
when love flings wide the door!
The family united;
the table filled once more.
The mother and the father,
the grandfolks all content.
Oh, little Child of Bethlehem,
all this your coming meant.

EDGAR A. GUEST

Let Us Keep Christmas

Whatever else be lost among the years,
Let us keep Christmas still a shining thing;
Whatever doubts assail us, or what fears,
Let us hold close one day, remembering
Its poignant meaning for the hearts of men.
Let us get back our childlike faith again.

Wealth may have taken wings, yet still there are
Clear windowpanes to glow with candlelight;
There are boughs for garlands, and a tinsel star
To tip some little fir tree's lifted height.
There is no heart too heavy or too sad,
But some small gift of love can make it glad.

And there are home-sweet rooms where laughter rings,
And we can sing the carols as of old.
Above the eastern hills a white star swings;
There is an ancient story to be told;
There are kind words and cheering words to say.
Let us be happy on the Christ Child's day.

GRACE NOLL CROWELL

Home for Christmas

ELIZABETH BOWEN

This is meeting-time again. Home is the magnet. The winter land roars and hums with the eager speed of return journeys. The dark is noisy and bright with late-night arrivals—doors thrown open, running shadows on snow, open arms, kisses, voices and laughter, laughter at everything and nothing. Inarticulate, giddying and confused are those original minutes of being back again. The very familiarity of everything acts like shock. Contentment has to be drawn in slowly, steadyingly, in deep breaths, there is so much of it. We rely on home not to change, and it does not, wherefore we give thanks. Again Christmas: abiding point of return. Set apart by its mystery, mood and magic, the season seems in a way to stand outside time. All that is dear, that is lasting, renews its hold on us: we are home again. . . .

This glow of Christmas, has it not in it also the gold of a harvest? "They shall return with joy, bringing their sheaves with them." To the festival, to each other, we bring in wealth. More to tell, more to understand, more to share. Each we have garnered in yet another year, to be glad, to celebrate to the full, we are come together. How akin we are to each other, how speechlessly dear and one in the fundamentals of being, Christmas shows us. No other time grants us, quite, this vision—round the tree or gathered before the fire we perceive anew, with joy, one another's faces. And each time faces come to mean more.

Is it not one of the mysteries of life that life should, after all, be so simple? Yes, as simple as Christmas, simple as this. Journeys through the dark to a lighted door, arms open. Laughter-smothered kisses, kiss-smothered laughter. And blessedness in the heart of it all. Here are the verities, all made gay with tinsel! Dear, silly Christmas-card saying and cracker mottoes—let them speak! Or, since still we cannot speak, let us sing! Dearer than memory, brighter than expectation is the ever returning now of Christmas. Why else, each time we greet its return, should happiness ring out in us like a peal of bells?

The Christmas Hearth

Now is the hour when glowing flames
Are leaping high above the hearth,
When firelight blossoms in the night,
And love encircles every heart.

The room is bright with happiness,
With holly boughs and fragrant pine,
With the spirit of abounding love
Amidst the glow of candle shine.

And wonder gleams beneath the tree
To captivate the very young,
While dear ones sit in quiet peace
Beside the fire, where dreams are spun.

A little warmth of love and cheer,
A roundelay of Christmas songs,
Can only weave an hour of joy
Before the blaze that lingers on.

The home fire with its subtle spell
Is fashioning a lovely light,
A warmer comfort to the hearts
Who gather by the fire tonight.

JOY BELLE BURGESS

Tell Me a Story of Christmas

BILL VAUGHN

It is good to be children sometimes, and never better than at Christmastime. —CHARLES DICKENS

"Tell me a story of Christmas," she said. The television mumbled faint inanities in the next room. From a few houses down the block came the sound of car doors slamming and guests being greeted with large cordiality.

Her father thought awhile. His mind went back over the interminable parade of Christmas books he had read at the bedside of his children.

"Well," he started tentatively, "once upon a time, it was the week before Christmas, all little elves at the North Pole were sad. . ."

"I'm tired of elves," she whispered. And he could tell she was tired, maybe almost as weary as he was himself after the last few feverish days.

"Okay," he said. "There was once, in a city not very far from here, the cutest wriggly little puppy you ever saw. The snow was falling, and this little puppy didn't have a home. As he walked along the streets, he saw a house that looked quite a bit like our house. And at the window—"

"Was a little girl who looked quite a bit like me," she said with a sigh. "I'm tired of puppies. I love Pinky, of course. I mean story puppies."

"Okay," he said. "No puppies. This narrows the field."

"What?"

"Nothing. I'll think of something. Oh, sure. There was a forest, way up in the north, farther even than where Uncle Ed lives. And all the trees were talking about how each one was going to be the grandest Christmas tree of all. One said, 'I'm going to be a Christmas tree too.' And all the trees laughed and laughed and said: 'A Christmas tree? You? Who would want you?'"

"No trees, Daddy," she said. "We have a tree at school and at Sunday school and at the supermarket and downstairs and a little one in my room. I am very tired of trees."

"You are very spoiled," he said.

"Hmmmmm," she replied. "Tell me a Christmas story."

"Let's see. All the reindeer up at the North Pole were looking forward

to pulling Santa's sleigh. All but one, and he felt sad because—" He began with a jolly ring in his voice but quickly realized that this wasn't going to work either. His daughter didn't say anything; she just looked at him reproachfully.

"Tired of reindeer too?" he asked. "Frankly, so am I. How about Christmas on the farm when I was a little boy? Would you like to hear about how it was in the olden days, when my grandfather would heat up bricks and put them in the sleigh and we'd all go for a ride?"

"Yes, Daddy," she said obediently. "But not right now. Not tonight."

He was silent, thinking. His repertoire, he was afraid, was exhausted. She was quiet too. Maybe, he thought, I'm home free. Maybe she has gone to sleep.

"Daddy," she murmured. "Tell me a story of Christmas."

Then it was as though he could read the words, so firmly were they in his memory. Still holding her hand, he leaned back:

"And it came to pass in those days, that there went out a decree from Caesar Augustus, that all the world should be taxed. . . ."

Her hand tightened a bit in his, and he told her a story of Christmas.

Christmas Hearth

Home for Christmas

There's magic in the thought of it,
A thrill beyond compare,
With tonic for a weary heart
And balm for every care.
Home for Christmas!

The Christmas tree is lovelier,
The holly wreaths more fair;
There's joy and sweet contentment
And love and loved ones there.
Home for Christmas!

The family cords seem tighter too,
And friendships more sincere,
While worldly things are cast aside
And home grows doubly dear.
Home for Christmas!

The road to Bethlehem seems near,
The star more brightly gleams;

The songs and carols sweetly sound,
Come true my fondest dreams . . .
Home for Christmas!

Though duties lead me far away
As I life's pathways climb,
There's no place like my Home Sweet Home,
Yes, home at Christmastime.
Home for Christmas!

Fragrant baking in the kitchen,
Gay gifts planned for sure delight,
The church bazaars and suppers,
And the programs Christmas night!
Home for Christmas!

The chimes that ring from steeples
Make hearts swell with joy unique.
Ah, the best thing I could wish for you
Is to go home for Christmas week.
Home for Christmas!

ESTHER LLOYD DAUBER

Home for Christmas

A little town at Christmas
 Is a page from yesteryear
When weary city-dwellers come
 To bask in love and cheer.

Every neighbor in the village
 Knows that Joe and Bill will come;
The sharing of the family news
 Makes happy heartstrings hum.

The trimming of the fragrant tree,
 The carols of the star,
The greeting of the old-time friends
 Make hometowns what they are.

A basket for the needy,
 Everyone knows where it goes . . .
So fill it high with goodies
 Till the Christmas spirit shows!

Fragrant baking in the kitchen;
 Gay gifts planned for sure delight;
The church bazaars and suppers
 And the programs Christmas night!

The chimes that ring from steeples
 Make hearts swell with joy unique.
Ah, the best thing I could wish you
 Is . . . go home for Christmas week!

LOLITA PINNEY

Christmas in the Heart

To Bethlehem our hearts, star led
 From wanderings far and wild,
Turn to a lowly cattle-shed
 And kneel before the Child.

We come from deserts, pitiless
 With only human pride;
And from the howling wilderness
 Where dread and hate abide.

Touched by His hand we find
 release from heavy griefs and fears:
Our hearts are lifted up with peace
 And purified by tears.

Ah Saviour dear! Thou Holy Child,
 What power is Thine to heal
Our broken hearts, our wills, defiled,
 When at Thy feet we kneel.

Grant us Thy grace no more to roam,
 But, following Thee alway,
Find Bethlehem in every home,
 The whole year Christmas Day.

AUTHOR UNKNOWN

An Orange in Our Stockings

Fred L. Holmes

The things I remember are not unusual. Mother strung a long rope across the living room on which we all hung our stockings. We had a Christmas tree also. We were sent upstairs early but went back down quietly on the stairs and tried to peep at them as they put up the presents.

Next morning an orange in one's stocking, along with candy and popcorn, was the greatest treat. For with no fruit stores as we now have them, oranges were to be found in the stores only at Christmastime. An orange for Christmas! That was something to remember and feel proud of having received! It was something worth telling to your playmates.

Christmas Eve services were held in the old Methodist church, and when we were older we were allowed to go along. I recall that inside the edifice were two long stoves—one on each side—filled with burning cordwood, from which ran stovepipes the full length of the church. Suspended by wires from the ceiling under the stovepipe joints were quart tin pails to catch the liquid soot that dripped. Light thrown into the church by silvered reflectors fastened to the wall behind the kerosene lamps gave all the light that was needed.

At the front of the church stood a large candlelighted Christmas tree for the Sunday School, but it was loaded with presents for the grownups as well. When the program carols had been sung the presents were distributed. Popcorn and candy were given out to the congregation, and the older children scrambled to capture the loops of popcorn and apples that decorated the tree. In those days everybody came to the church festivities in horse-drawn bobsleighs. With straw in the bottom of the sleigh box, soapstones at our feet, and covered with buffalo robes, we were kept warm for the ride. During the exercises the horses were heavily blanketed; at the end they were frisky as they sensed the imminence of the trip back to the farm barn.

It's Christmas Stocking Time

Do you recall,
When you were small,
What gave you so much pleasure?
I remember Christmas Day;
Santa filled stockings gay
With unexpected treasure.

Limp socks in a row
Would steal the show
All through Christmas night;
While eager anticipation
And wild exhilaration
Filled our hearts with keen delight.

There they hung,
Lifeless and unsung,
Till Santa would fill them all;
To bed we went,
Our energy spent,
Waiting eagerly for his call.

Though we hardly slept,
The hours slowly crept
Till Christmas morn arrived.
Then out of bed
With full speed ahead,
Excitedly we cried.

What a thrill!
Our hearts had their fill
As we spied each knobby sock.
We'll always treasure
The memory and pleasure
As around them we all would flock.

Let's keep alive
The joy we derive
From magic that Christmas can bestow.
Oh heart, never grow old
As you enfold
Memories of Christmas stockings in a row.

ANN SCHNEIDER

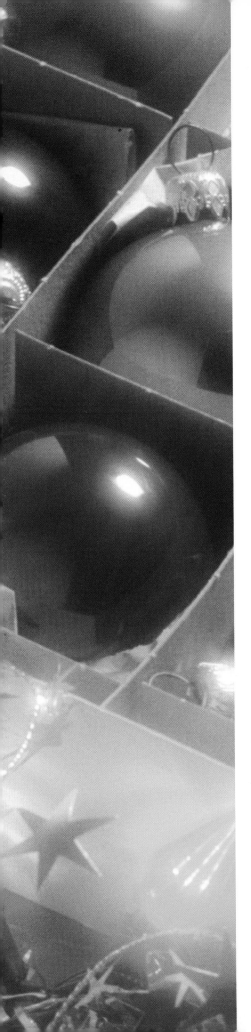

Gathering Round

AUTHOR UNKNOWN

At a signal from my mother we followed her into the dining room on the other side of the passage. Here a sight awaited us that surprised us one and all. The room was brilliantly lighted up with wax candles on sconces from the walls; and on the table in the center there was placed a great Christmas tree, hung all over with little lamps and bon-bons, and toys and sweetmeats and bags of cakes. It was the first tree of the kind that I and my companions had ever seen. It was quite a new-fashion, the Christmas tree; and my brother Tom, who had just come home from Germany, had superintended its getting up and decoration. With what shouts of joy we hailed the pretty Christmas tree, and with what glee and laughter we began to search among its twinkling lights and bright green leaves for the toys and sweetmeats that were hanging there, each one with a name written on its envelope, I can hardly tell you. But we were very merry, I know, and very grateful to our dear mother for her care in providing this delightful surprise as a finish to our merry evening's sports.

Christmas Ornaments

The boxes break
At the corners,
Their sides
Sink weak;

They are tied up
Every year
With the same
Gray string;

But under the split
Lids, a fortune
Shines: globes
Of gold and sapphire,

Silver spires and
Bells, jeweled
Nightingales with
Pearly tails.

VALERIE WORTH

Come Christmas

You see this Christmas tree all silver gold?
It stood out many winters in the cold,

with tinsel sometimes made of crystal ice,
say once a winter morning—maybe twice.

More often it was trimmed by fallen snow
so heavy that the branches bent, with no

one anywhere to see how wondrous is
the hand of God in that white world of his.

And if you think it lonely through the night
when Christmas trees in houses take the light,

remember how his hand put up one star
in this same sky so long ago afar.

All stars are hung so every Christmas tree
has one above it. Let's go out and see.

DAVID MCCORD

The Voice of the Christ-Child

The earth has grown cold with its burden of care,
But at Christmas it always is young.
The heart of the jewel burns lustrous and fair,
And its soul full of music breaks forth on the air,
When the song of the Angels is sung.

It is coming, old earth, it is coming tonight;
On the snowflakes which cover thy sod,
The feet of the Christ-child fall gently and white,
And the voice of the Christ-child tells out with delight
That mankind are the children of God.

PHILLIPS BROOKS

And for as Long as I Can Remember

CATHERINE OTTEN

At Christmas all roads lead home.
—MARJORIE HOLMES

Mama wasn't stingy—far from it, but I never saw her spend a dime. When we were young, I suppose we didn't notice her thrifty quirk, but as we grew up, we all worried about Mama's concern with dimes.

Mama ran our house like a tight little ship. She and Papa set the course for their young crew, which was made up of my two sisters, my two brothers, and me.

The term "good old days" could have originated in our home. Mama never ran out of energy or food, and we seldom ate Sunday suppers alone. Unexpected company usually dropped in, and there was always enough food to go around. Mama's Saturday baking binge took care of that. Little did we youngsters know or care that those were the days of the Depression. But we never felt deprived.

Years slipped by, and one by one we left home to start families of our own. When Papa retired, he and Mama moved into our summer cottage.

During our visits, we became more aware of Mama's obsession with dimes. When we shopped with her, she refused to use a single dime even if it meant breaking a dollar bill to pay for a ten-cent item. What was wrong with our mother?

"Well, let her have her dimes," I thought. "I save grease until I run out of containers, only to throw it all out and start filling those empty jars again."

Christmas was the time we all gathered for a big family dinner. Mama would have it no other way.

"Dinner is at four o'clock," Mama would say. "Just bring yourselves, and don't be late."

Dad would be busy for weeks making wreaths from the pine trees in the yard. One Christmas every window boasted a small wreath, and a huge one decorated the door.

By the time the last family arrived with their treasures, the pile of gifts resembled a pyramid, competing in height and beauty with the shining Christmas tree.

The Christmas dinner table was another picture that we shall never forget. It had been pulled out into the living room, and stretched to its full length. The shining dishes and silverware had been polished to the hilt for the occasion.

The centerpiece was always the same—little wax candle skaters, snowmen, angels, animals, and trees carefully placed on the raised round reflector. The sparkling water goblets resembled a picket fence around the relish dishes, salads, cranberries, biscuits, mints, and nuts.

The hot dishes were brought in with ceremony. The huge, golden-brown turkey was placed in front of Papa. Then came platters of buttery vegetables and heaping bowls of mashed and sweet potatoes. Papa led grace as our eyes feasted on the picture before us. We toasted everyone's welfare in the coming year, and the feast began. One Christmas as we put away the dishes and the leftovers, we girls ganged up on Mama and insisted on sharing the expenses of the day. She was quiet for a bit, and then she revealed her secret.

"Don't worry, children," she laughed. I pay for it all with a year of dimes that I've saved."

We looked at each other guiltily. Our concern

over Mama's thing with dimes melted into relief. The joke was on us!

Years have passed since that Christmas. Now my children are grown and raising families of their own, passing on the traditions that our parents gave to us.

Papa and I think of Christmas as "our day," and we try to create the same happy time that our parents made for us. Now I see my daughters fussing and whispering about my eccentricities.

"You should see the jars of grease in Mother's refrigerator," I overheard Cathy tell a friend one day. "And for as long as I can remember, Mama never spent a dime!"

A Christmas Feast

Christmas Dinner

The heart remembers Christmas
And days of long ago,
When festive preparations
Made all the house aglow;
The kitchen fairly bubbled
With turkey, puddings, pies,
And all those extra goodies
Which came as a surprise.

Each person had his duties,
And old and young could share;
The little ones and Grandma
And even "Sport" were there;

The fruitcake and the mincemeat,
The chestnut dressing too,
The pumpkins and red apples
Filled childhood's world anew.

Yes hearts go home at Christmas
To take again their place,
To see at Christmas dinner
Each dear, remembered face;
And though the scene we cherish
A short while will be there,
The words, the joy, the laughter,
Are with us everywhere!

ALICE KENNELLY ROBERTS

Cornbread and Sausage Stuffing

12 tablespoons unsalted butter, divided	3 cups cubed dry white bread
2½ cups finely chopped yellow onions	2 teaspoons dried thyme
3 tart apples, cored and chopped; do not peel	1 teaspoon dried sage
1 pound bulk breakfast sausage	½ cup chopped fresh parsley
3 cups cubed dry cornbread	1½ cups chopped pecans
3 cups cubed dry whole-wheat bread	Salt and pepper to taste

In a skillet, melt 6 tablespoons butter; add yellow onion. Cook over medium heat until golden. Pour onions and butter into a large mixing bowl. Melt an additional 6 tablespoons of butter in the skillet; add apples. Cook over high heat only until just beginning to color but not mushy. Add to onions. Crumble sausage into the skillet and fry until lightly browned. Remove sausage with a slotted spoon and drain. Add sausage and remaining ingredients to onion mixture. Toss to mix. Refrigerate to cool completely before stuffing turkey or spoon into a 3-quart casserole. Cover and bake at 325° F. for 30 to 45 minutes. Baste occasionally with chicken broth. Makes enough stuffing for a 20-pound turkey or 12 to 14 servings.

Cranberry and Apple Relish

1 pound fresh cranberries	1½ cups granulated sugar
2 medium apples, washed and cored; do not peel	½ teaspoon ground ginger
2 teaspoons orange zest	½ teaspoon ground cinnamon
2 tablespoons lemon juice	¼ teaspoon ground cloves

Put cranberries and apples through a food grinder or grind in food processor. Stir in orange zest, lemon juice, sugar, ginger, cinnamon, and cloves. Chill in a covered jar overnight for flavors to blend. Makes 3½ cups.

Christmas
GATHERINGS

The Holly and the Ivy

TRADITIONAL

OLD FRENCH CAROL

1. The hol - ly and the i - vy, when
2. The hol - ly bears a blos - som, white
3. The hol - ly bears a ber - ry, as
4. The hol - ly bears a prick - le, as

they were both full grown, Of all the trees that are
as the lil - y flower, And Ma - ry bore sweet
red as an - y blood, And Ma - ry bore sweet
sharp as an - y thorn, And Ma - ry bore sweet

in the wood, the hol - ly bears the crown.
Je - sus Christ, to be our sweet Sav - iour.
Je - sus Christ, to do poor sin - ners good.
Je - sus Christ, on Christ - mas in the morn.

Journey into Christmas

Bess Streeter Aldrich

Welcome . . . to your shelter underneath the holly, to your places 'round the Christmas fire.—Charles Dickens

Margaret Staley stood at her library window looking out at the familiar elms and the lace-vine arbor. Tonight the trees were snow-crusted, the arbor a thing of crystal filigree under the Christmas stars.

Some years the Midwest stayed mild all through December, donning its snowsuit only after the holidays. But tonight was a Christmas Eve made to order, as though Nature had supervised the designing and decorating of a silvered stage setting.

Margaret Staley visualized all this perfection, but she knew that the very beauty of the scene brought into sharper contrast the fact that for the first time in her life she was alone on Christmas Eve.

For fifty-nine Christmases she had been surrounded by the people she loved. On this sixtieth, there was no one. For not one of her four children was coming home.

The reasons for none of the four coming were all good. Three of the reasons were, anyway, she admitted reluctantly. Calling the roll she went over, for the hundredth time, why each could not make the trip.

Don. That was understandable. Don and Janet, his wife, and young Ralph in California could not be expected to come half way across the continent every year, and they had been here last Christmas. She herself had visited them the past summer, returning as late as September.

Ruth. Ruth was her career daughter, connected with a children's hospital and vitally important to her post. Long ago she had accepted the fact that Ruth could give her only the fragments from a busy life and never had she begrudged it; indeed, she had felt vicariously a part of her capable daughter's service to humanity.

Jean. Jeanie and her husband, Roy, lived in Chicago. Jeanie was a great family girl and certainly would have come out home, but the two little boys were in quarantine.

Lee. The hurt which she had loyally pushed into the back of her mind jumped out again like an unwanted and willful jack-in-the-box. Lee and his Ann could have come.

Living in Oklahoma, not too far away, they could have made the trip if they had wished. Or if it had not been convenient for Lee to leave, she could have gone down there to be with them. *If they had asked her.*

The only time Christmas had been mentioned was in a letter, now several weeks old. Lee had mentioned casually that they were going to have company for Christmas. That would be Ann's folks of course. You mustn't be selfish. You had to remember that there were in-laws to be taken into consideration.

Standing there at the window, looking out at the silver night, she remembered how she once thought the family would always come home. In her younger years she had said complacently, "I know my children. They love their old home and whenever possible they will spend Christmas in it. Of course there will be sickness and other reasons to keep them away at times, but some of the four will always be here." And surprisingly it had been true. Someone had been here every Christmas.

Faintly into her reveries came the far-off sound of bells and she opened the casement window a bit to locate their tinkling. It was the carolers, carrying out the town's traditional singing on Christmas Eve.

She closed the window and drew the drapes, as though unable to bear the night's white beauty and the poignant notes of young voices.

"I'm alone . . . I'm alone . . . it's Christmas Eve and I'm alone." Her mind repeated it like some mournful raven with its "nevermore."

Suddenly she caught herself by a figurative grip. "Now, listen," she said to that self which was grieving. "You are not a weak person and you're not neurotic. You have good sense and understanding and even humor at times. How often have you criticized people for this very thing?"

She walked over to the radio and turned, it on, but when "Silent Night . . . Holy Night", came softly forth, she snapped it off, afraid she would break down and weep like an old Niobe.

"Oh, go on . . . feel sorry for yourself if you want to. Go on. Do it." She smiled again wryly, and knew she was trying to clutch at humor, that straw which more than once had saved her from drowning in troubled waters.

She went over to her desk and got out the four last letters from the children, although she knew their contents thoroughly.

She put the letters away and went into the living room. It looked as big as Grand Central Station. Last year there had been eleven sitting in these chairs which tonight were as empty as her heart. Half ashamed at her childishness in trying to create an illusion, she began pulling them out to form the semicircle of last year when the big tree had been its pivotal point. She could even recall where each had sat that morning at the opening of the gifts. Jeanie and Bud on the davenport, Ruth curled up on the hassock, Ann and Lee side by side in the big blue chairs—and on around the circle.

She had to smile again to remember the red rocking-chair which she brought from the storeroom for young Larry. It had been her own little rocker and was fifty-eight years old. A brown tidy cushion hung limply on its cane back, an old-fashioned piece worked in cross-stitch, the faded red letters reading: FOR MARGARET. Larry had squeezed into it, but when his name was called and he rose excitedly to get his first present, the chair rose with him and they had to pry him out of it and one of the chair's arms cracked. There had been so much hilarious laughter where tonight was only silence. And silence can be so very much louder than noise.

With the chairs forming their ghost-like semicircle beside her, she turned her own around to the fireplace and sat down to give herself the pleasure and the pain of remembering old Christmases. Swiftly her

mind traversed the years, darting from one long gone holiday season to another.

The Christmas before Don was born she and John were in their first new home. They had been very happy that year, just the two of them; so happy in fact that she had felt almost conscience stricken to think she could be contented without her own old family at holiday time.

Then Don's first Christmas when he was eleven months old. After these thirty-six years she could still remember how he clutched a big glass marble and would not notice anything else. Strange how such small details stayed in one's mind.

The Christmas before Jeanie was born, when she did not go out to shop, but sent for her gifts by mail, so that the opening of them was almost as much a surprise to her as to the recipients.

Then there was the whooping-cough Christmas, with the house full of medicated steam and all four youngsters dancing and whooping spasmodically around the tree like so many little Indians.

There was the time she bought the big doll for Ruth and when it proved to have a large paint blemish on its leg, she wanted to return it for a perfect one. But Ruth would not hear of it and made neat little bandages for the leg as though it were a wound. It was the first she ever noticed Ruth's nursing instincts.

Dozens of memories flocked to her mind. There had not always been happy holidays. Some of them were immeasurably sad. Darkest of all was the one after John's death, with the children trying to carry out cheerfully the old family customs, knowing that it was what Dad would have wanted. But even in the troubled days there had been warm companionship to share the burden, not this icy loneliness.

For a few moments she sat, unmoving, lost in the memory of that time, then aroused herself to continue her mental journeying.

Soon after that Christmas was no longer a childish affair. Gifts suddenly ceased to be skates and hockey-sticks and became sorority party dresses and fraternity rings, and the house was full of young people home for vacation. Then the first marriage and Don's Janet was added to the circle, then Jeanie brought Roy into it. In time the first grandson, and another, and a third—all the youthful pleasure of the older members of the family renewed through the children's eyes.

Then came that Christmas when the blast of the ships in their harbor had sent its detonations here into this very living room, as into every one in the country. And though all were here and tried to be natural and merry, only the children were free from forebodings of what the next year would bring. And it brought many changes: Don with his Reserves, Roy enlisting in the Navy, Lee in the Army. That was the year they expected Lee home from the nearby camp. His presents were under the tree and the Christmas Eve dinner ready, only to have him phone that his leave had been canceled, so that the disappointment was keener than if they had not expected him at all.

Then those dark holiday times with all three boys overseas and Jean and the babies living here at home. Ruth in uniform, coming for one Christmas, calm and clear-eyed as always, realizing perhaps more than the others that at home or abroad,

waking or sleeping, death holds us always in the hollow of his hand.

Then the clouds beginning to lift and, one by one, all coming back, Lee the last to arrive. And that grand reunion of last year after all the separations and the fears. All safe. All home. The warm touch of the hand and the welcoming embrace. Pretty Ann added to the circle. The decorating of the tree. The lights in the window. The darting in and out for last minute gift wrapping. The favorite recipes. Old songs resung. Old family jokes retold. Old laughter renewed. In joy and humility she had said, "My cup runneth over."

Recalling all this, she again grew stern with herself. How could one ask for anything more after that safe return and perfect reunion? But the contrast between then and tonight was too great. All her hopes had ended in loneliness. All her fears of approaching age had become true. One could not help the deep depression. The head may tell the heart all sorts of sensible things, but at Christmastime the heart is stronger.

She sat for a long time in front of the fire which had not warmed her. She had been on a long emotional journey, and it had left her tired and spent.

From the library, loud and brazen, the phone rang. It startled her for she had never outgrown her fear of a late call. With her usual trepidation she hastened to answer. There was some delay, a far off operator's voice, and then Lee.

"That you, Mother?"

"Yes, Lee, yes. How are you?"

"Fine. Did Jeanie come?"

"No, the boys are still quarantined."

"Ruth?"

"No."

"You there alone?"

"Yes."

"Gosh, that's too bad on the old family night. Well, cheer up. I've got news for you. Our company came. She weighs seven pounds and fourteen ounces."

"What . . . what did you say, Lee?"

"Our daughter arrived, Mom. Four hours ago. I waited at the hospital to see that Ann was all right."

"Why, Lee, you never told . . . we never knew . . ."

"It was Ann's idea of a good joke. And listen, we've named her Margaret—for you, Mother. Do you like it?"

"Why, yes . . . yes, I do like it, Lee."

There was more, sometimes both talking at once and having to repeat. Then Lee saying, "We were wondering if you could come down in a couple of weeks. Ann thinks she'd like to have an old hand at the business around. Can you arrange it?"

"Oh, yes, Lee . . . I'm sure I could."

"Good. Well, I'll hang up now. Spent enough on my call . . . have to save my money to send Margaret to college. Be seeing you."

"Lee . . ." In those last seconds she wanted desperately to put into words all the things her heart was saying. But you cannot put the thoughts garnered from a life of love and service into a sentence. So she only said: "Be a good dad, Lee. Be as good a dad as . . ." She broke off, but he understood.

"I know. I'll try. Merry Christmas, Mom."

"Merry Christmas, Lee."

She put down the receiver and walked into the living room, walked briskly as though to tell her news, her heart beating with pleasant excitement. The semicircle of chairs confronted her. With physical sight she saw their emptiness. But, born of love and imagination, they were all occupied as plainly as ever eyes had seen them. She had a warm sense of companionship. The house seemed alive with humans. How could they be so real? She swept the circle with that second sight which had been given her. Don over there . . . Ruth on the hassock . . .

Jeanie on the davenport . . . Lee and Ann in the big blue chairs . . .

Suddenly she turned and walked hurriedly down the hall to the closet and came back with the little red chair. She pushed the two blue chairs apart and set the battered rocker between them. On the back hung the old brown tidy with its red cross-stitching: FOR MARGARET.

She smiled at it happily. All her numbness of spirit had vanished, her loneliness gone. This was a good Christmas. Why, this was one of the best Christmases she ever had!

She felt a sudden desire to go back to the library, to look out at the silvery garden and up to the stars. That bright one up there—it must be the one that stops over all cradles.

Faintly she could hear bells and voices. That would be the young crowd coming back from their caroling, so she opened the window again.

Oh, little town of Bethlehem,
How still we see thee lie . . .

The words came clearly across the starlit snow, singing themselves into her consciousness with a personal message:

Yet in thy dark streets shineth
The everlasting light
The hopes and fears of all the years
Are met in thee tonight.

The hopes and fears of all the years! She felt the old Christmas lift of the heart, that thankfulness and joy she had always experienced when the children were all together . . . all well . . . all home.

"My cup runneth over."

At the door of the living room she paused to turn off the lights. Without looking toward the circle of chairs, so there might come no disillusion, she said over her shoulder:

"Good-night, children. Merry Christmas. See you early in the morning."

While the Christmas Log Is Burning

Hail to the night when we gather once more
All the forms we love to meet;
When we've many a guest that's dear to our breast;
And the household dog at our feet.
Who would not be in the circle of glee,
When heart to heart is yearning—
When joy breathes out in the laughing shout
While the Christmas log is burning?

'Tis one of the fairy hours of life,
When the world seems all of light;
For the thought of woe or the name of a foe
Ne'er darkens the festive night.
When bursting mirth rings round the hearth,
Oh where is the spirit, that's mourning;
While merry bells chime with the carol rhyme,
And the Christmas log is burning?

Then is the time when the gray old man
Leaps back to the days of youth;
When brows and eyes bear no disguise,
But flush and gleam with truth.
Oh then is the time when the soul exults,
And seems right heavenward turning;
When we love and bless the hands we press,
While the Christmas log is burning.

ELIZA COOK

Deck the Hall

Deck the hall with boughs of holly,
Fa la la la la, la la la la.
'Tis the season to be jolly,
Fa la la la la, la la la la.

Don we now our gay apparel,
Fa la la la la, la la la la.
Troll the ancient Yuletide carol,
Fa la la la la, la la la la.

See the blazing Yule before us,
Fa la la la la, la la la la.
Strike the harp and join the chorus.
Fa la la la la, la la la la.

Follow me in merry measure,
Fa la la la la, la la la la.
While I tell of Yuletide treasure,
Fa la la la la, la la la la.

Fast away the old year passes,
Fa la la la la, la la la la.
Hail the new, ye lads and lasses,
Fa la la la la, la la la la.

Sing we joyous, all together,
Fa la la la la, la la la la.
Heedless of the wind and weather,
Fa la la la la, la la la la.

TRADITIONAL WELSH CAROL

Christmas Delights

Apple-Raisin Crisp

1¼ cups old-fashioned oats

1 cup plus 2 tablespoons firmly packed brown sugar

¾ cup plus 1 tablespoon all-purpose flour, divided

1 teaspoon ground cinnamon, divided

¼ teaspoon salt

¾ cup unsalted butter

¾ cup chopped walnuts

4 pounds Granny Smith apples; peeled, cored, and sliced

1½ cups golden raisins

½ cup granulated sugar

1 tablespoon fresh lemon juice

Preheat oven to 375°F. Butter a 9-x 13½-inch baking dish. In a large bowl, combine oats, brown sugar, ¾ cup flour, ¼ teaspoon cinnamon, and salt. Cut in butter until coarse crumbs form. Stir in chopped walnuts. Set aside. In a large bowl, combine apples, raisins, sugar, lemon juice, 1 tablespoon flour, and ¾ teaspoon cinnamon. Mix well to blend. Pour apple-raisin mixture into prepared dish. Sprinkle oats mixture over top. Bake 55 minutes or until topping is golden brown. Serve warm with scoops of vanilla ice cream. Makes 8 servings.

The Time Has Come

Now that the time has come
Wherein our Saviour Christ was born,
The larder's full of beef and pork,
The granary's full of corn.

As God hath plenty to thee sent,
Take comfort of thy labors,
And let it never thee repent,
To feast thy needy neighbors.

AUTHOR UNKNOWN

Pumpkin-Raisin Bread

2	envelopes active dry yeast		2	large eggs, lightly beaten
½	cup warm water		1½	teaspoons ground cardamom
1	cup whole milk		2	teaspoons ground ginger
½	cup butter		2	teaspoons salt
½	cup granulated sugar		8½	cups sifted all-purpose flour
1	cup cooked mashed pumpkin		1½	cups raisins

Soften dry yeast in warm water and set aside in a warm place. Scald milk; remove from heat and add butter and sugar. Stir to dissolve butter; cool to lukewarm. Stir in yeast mixture, pumpkin, and eggs. Add cardamom, ginger, and salt. Add flour along with raisins. Turn out onto a floured board. Knead in remaining flour until about half of the dough is smooth and satiny. Form into a ball; place in a greased bowl, turning once to grease top. Cover and let rise in a warm place until doubled in size.

Lightly grease two 9-x 5-x 3-inch loaf pans. Punch dough down and turn out onto a lightly floured board. Lightly knead half the dough and form it into an oblong. Place into prepared pan. Repeat with remaining dough. Brush tops with melted butter. Cover and let rise in a warm place until doubled in bulk. Preheat oven to 375° F. Bake 45 minutes or until top is golden. Serve warm or wrap tightly in plastic and let flavors ripen overnight.

Mrs. Brownlow's Christmas Party

WILLIS BOYD ALLEN

Great is the spirit of Christmas that brings to every heart peace, goodwill toward all mankind. —HORACE WILSON

It was fine Christmas weather. Several light snowstorms in the early part of December had left the earth fair and white, and the sparkling, cold days that followed were enough to make the most crabbed and morose of mankind cheerful, as with a foretaste of the joyous season at hand. Downtown, the sidewalks were crowded with mothers and sisters, buying gifts for their sons, brothers, and husbands.

Among those who were looking forward to the holidays with keen anticipations of pleasure were Mr. and Mrs. Brownlow of Elm Street, Boston. They had quietly talked the matter over together, and decided that, as there were three children in the family (not counting themselves, as they might well have done), it would be a delightful and not too expensive luxury to give a little Christmas party.

"You see, John," said Mrs. Brownlow, "we've been asked, ourselves, to half a dozen candy-pulls and parties since we've lived here, and it seems nothin' but fair that we should do it once ourselves."

"That's so, Clarissy," replied her husband slowly; "but then there's so many of us, and my salary's, well, it would cost considerable, little woman, wouldn't it?"

"I'll tell you what!" she exclaimed. "We needn't have a regular grown-up party, but just one for children. We can get a small tree and a bit of a present for each of the boys and girls, with ice cream and cake, and let it go at that. The whole thing sha'n't cost ten dollars."

"Good!" said Mr. Brownlow heartily. "I knew you'd get some way out of it. Let's tell Bob and Sue and Polly, so they can have the fun of looking forward to it."

So it was settled and all hands entered into the plan with such a degree of earnestness that one would have thought these people were going to have some grand gift themselves, instead of giving to others and pinching for a month afterwards in their own comforts, as they knew they would have to do.

The first real difficulty they met was in deciding whom to invite. John was for asking only the children of their immediate neighbors; but Mrs. Brownlow said it would be a kindness, as well as polite, to include those who were better off than themselves.

"I allus think, John," she explained, laying her hand on his shoulder, "that it's just's much despisin' to look down on your rich neighbors—as if all they'd got was money—as on your poor ones. Let's ask 'em all: Deacon Holsum's, the Brights, and the Nortons." The Brights were Mr. Brownlow's employers.

"Anybody else?" queried her husband, with his funny twinkle. "P'raps you'd like to have me ask the governor's family!"

"Now, John, don't you be saucy," she laughed, relieved at having carried her point. "Let's put our heads together, and see who to set down. Susie will write the notes in her nice hand, and Bob can deliver them to save postage."

"Well, you've said three," counted Mr. Brownlow on his fingers. "Then there's Mrs. Sampson's little girl, and the four Williamses, and"—he enumerated one family after another, till nearly thirty names were on the list.

Once Susie broke in, "Oh Pa, *don't* invite that Mary Spenfield she's awfully stuck-up and cross!"

"Good!" said her father again. "This will be just the thing for her. Let her be coffee and you be sugar, and see how much you can sweeten her that evening."

In the few days that intervened before the twenty-fifth, the whole family were busy enough: Mrs. Brownlow shopping, Susie writing the notes, and the others helping wherever they got a chance. Every evening they spread out upon the sitting-room floor such presents as had been bought during the day. These were not costly, but they were chosen lovingly, and seemed very nice indeed to Mr. Brownlow and the children, who united in praising the discriminating taste of Mrs. B.

The tree seemed at first inclined to be sulky, perhaps at having been decapitated and curtailed; for it obstinately leaned backward, kicked over the soap-box in which it was set, bumped against Mr. Brownlow, tumbled forward, and in short, behaved itself like a tree which was determined to lie on its precious back all the next day, or perish in the attempt. At length, just as they were beginning to despair of ever getting it firm and straight, it gave a little quiver of its limbs, yielded gracefully to a final push by Bob, and stood upright, as fair and comely a Christmas tree as one would wish to see. Mr. Brownlow crept out backward from under the lower branches, and regarded it with a sigh of content. Such presents as were to be disposed of in this way were now hung upon the branches; then strings of popcorn, bits of wool, and glistening paper, a few red apples, and lastly the candies. When all was finished, which was not before midnight, the family withdrew to their beds, with weary limbs and brains, but with lighthearted anticipation of tomorrow.

"Do you s'pose Mrs. Bright will come with her children, John?" asked Mrs. Brownlow, as she turned out the gas.

"Shouldn't wonder"—sleepily from the four-poster.

"Did Mr. Bright say anything about the invitation we sent when he paid you off?"

Silence. More silence. Good Mr. Brownlow was asleep, and Clarissa soon followed him.

Meanwhile the snow, which had been falling fast during the early part of the evening, had ceased, leaving the earth as fair to look upon as the fleece-drifted sky above it. Slowly the heavy banks of cloud rolled away, disclosing star after star, until the moon itself looked down and sent a soft "Merry Christmas" to mankind. At last came the dawn, with a glorious burst of sunlight and churchbells and glad voices, ushering in the gladdest and dearest day of all the year.

The Brownlows were early astir, full of the joyous spirit of the day. There was a clamor of Christmas greetings and a delighted medley of shouts from the children over the few simple gifts that had been secretly laid aside for them. But the ruling thought in every heart was the party. It was to come off at five o'clock in the afternoon, when it would be just dark enough to light the candles on the tree.

In spite of all the hard work of the preceding days, there was not a moment to spare that forenoon. The house, as the head of the family facetiously remarked, was a perfect hive of B's.

As the appointed hour drew near, their nervousness increased. Nor was the excitement confined to the interior of the house. The tree was placed in the front parlor, close to the window, and by half-past four a dozen ragged children were gathered about the iron fence of the little front yard, gazing open-mouthed and open-eyed at the spectacular wonders within. At a quarter before five Mrs. Brownlow's heart beat hard every time she heard a strange footstep in their quiet street. It was a little odd that none of the guests had arrived; but then, it was fashionable to be late!

Ten minutes more passed. Still no arrivals. It was evident that each was planning not to be the first to get there and that they would all descend on the house and assault the door-bell at once. Mrs. Brownlow repeatedly smoothed the wrinkles out of her tidy apron, and Mr. Brownlow began to perspire with responsibility.

Meanwhile, the crowd outside, recognizing no rigid

bonds of etiquette, rapidly increased in numbers. Mr. Brownlow, to pass the time and please the poor little homeless creatures, lighted two of the candles.

The response from the front-yard fence was immediate. A low murmur of delight ran along the line, and several dull-eyed babies were hoisted, in the arms of babies scarcely older than themselves, to behold the rare vision of candles in a tree, just illumining the further splendors glistening here and there among the branches.

The kind man's heart warmed towards them, and he lighted two more candles. The delight of the audience could now hardly be restrained, and the babies, having been temporarily lowered by the aching little arms of their respective nurses, were shot up once more to view the redoubled grandeur.

The whole family had become so much interested in these small outcasts that they had not noticed the flight of time. Now some one glanced suddenly at the clock, and exclaimed, "It's nearly half-past five!"

The Brownlows looked at one another blankly. Poor Mrs. Brownlow's smart ribbons drooped in conscious abasement, while mortification and pride struggled in their wearer's kindly face, over which, after a moment's silence, one large tear slowly rolled and dropped off.

Mr. Brownlow gave himself a little shake and sat down, as was his wont upon critical occasions. As his absent gaze wandered about the room, so prettily decked for the guests who didn't come, it fell upon a little worn, gilt-edged volume on the table. At that sight, a new thought occurred to him. "Clarissy," he said softly, going over to his wife and putting his arm around her, "Clarissy, seein's the well-off folks haven't accepted, don't you think we'd better

invite some of the others in?" And he pointed significantly toward the window.

Mrs. Brownlow, dispatching another tear after the first, nodded. She was not quite equal to words yet. Being a woman, the neglect of her little party cut her even more deeply than it did her husband.

Mr. Brownlow stepped to the front door. Nay more, he walked down the short flight of steps, took one little girl by the hand, and said in his pleasant, fatherly way,

"Wouldn't you like to go in and look at the tree? Come, Puss" (to the waif at his side), "we'll start first."

With these words he led the way back through the open door and into the warm, lighted room. The children hung back a little, but seeing that no harm came to the first guest, soon flocked in, each trying to keep behind all the rest, but at the same time shouldering the babies up into view as before.

In the delightful confusion that followed, the good hosts forgot all about the miscarriage of their plans. They completely outdid themselves, in efforts to please their hastily acquired company. Bob spoke a piece, the girls sang duets. Mrs. Brownlow had held every individual baby in her motherly arms before half an hour was over. And as for Mr. Brownlow, it was simply marvelous to see him go among those children, giving them the presents, and initiating their owners into the mysterious impelling forces of monkeys with yellow legs and gymnastic tendencies; filling the boys' pockets with popcorn, blowing horns and tin whistles; now assaulting the tree (it had been lighted throughout, and—bless it—how firm it stood now!) for fresh novelties, now diving into the kitchen and returning in an unspeakably cohesive state of breathlessness and molasses candy—all the while laughing, talking, patting heads, joking, until the kindly Spirit of Christmas Present would have wept and smiled at once, for the pleasure of the sight.

"And now, my young friends," said Mr. Brownlow, raising his voice, "we'll have a little ice cream in the back room. Women first, gentlemen afterward!" So saying, he gallantly stood side, with a sweep of his hand, to allow Mrs. Brownlow to precede him. But just as the words left his mouth there came a sharp ring at the door-bell.

"It's a carriage!" gasped Mrs. Brownlow, flying to the front window, and backing precipitately. "Susie, go to that door an' see who 'tis. Land sakes, what a mess this parlor's in!" And she gazed with a true housekeeper's dismay at the littered carpet and dripping candles.

"Deacon Holsum and Mrs. Hartwell, Pa!" announced Susie, throwing open the parlor door.

The lady thus mentioned came forward with outstretched hand. Catching a glimpse of Mrs. Brownlow's embarrassed face she exclaimed quickly.

"Isn't this splendid! Father and I were just driving past, and we saw your tree through the window, and couldn't resist dropping in upon you. You won't mind us, will you?"

"Mind—you," repeated Mrs. Brownlow in astonishment. "Why of course not, only you are so late we didn't expect . . ."

Mrs. Hartwell looked puzzled. "Pardon me. I don't think I quite understand."

"The invitation was for five, you know, ma'am."

"But we received no invitation!"

Mr. Brownlow, who had greeted the deacon heartily and then listened with amazement to this conversation, now turned upon Bob, with a signally futile attempt at a withering glance.

Bob looked as puzzled as the rest, for a moment. Then his face fell, and he flushed to the roots of his hair.

"I—I—must—have—forgotten," he stammered.

"Forgotten what?"

"The invitations—they're in my desk now!" Thus Bob, with utterly despairing tone and self-abasement.

"You poor dear!" Mrs. Hartwell cried, kissing her hostess, who stood speechless, not knowing whether to laugh or cry, "So that's why nobody came! But who has cluttered, who has been having such a good time here, then?"

Mr. Brownlow silently led the last two arrivals to the door of the next room, and pointed in. It was now the kind deacon's turn to be touched.

"Into the highways!" he murmured, as he looked upon the unwashed, hungry little circle about the table.

"I s'pose," said Mr. Brownlow, doubtfully, "they'd like to have you sit down with 'em, just's if they were folks, if you didn't mind?"

Mind! I wish you could have seen the rich furs and overcoat come off and go down on the floor in a heap before Polly could catch them!

Mr. Brownlow looked over to the deacon, and he asked a blessing on the little ones gathered there. "Thy servants, the masters of this house, have suffered them to come unto thee," he said in his prayer. "Wilt thou take them into thine arms, O Father of lights, and bless them."

A momentary hush followed, and then the fun began again. Sweetly and swiftly kind words flew back and forth across the table, each one carrying its own golden thread and weaving the hearts of poor and rich into the one fine fabric of brotherhood and humanity they were meant to form.

Outside, the snow began to fall once more, each crystaled flake whispering softly as it touched the earth that Christmas night, "Peace-peace!"

A Hint for Next Christmas

A. A. MILNE

What can I give Him, Poor as I am? If I were a shepherd I would bring a lamb, If I were a Wise Man, I would do my part; yet what I can give Him, Give my heart. ——CHRISTINA ROSSETTI

Obviously there should be a standard value for a certain type of Christmas present. One may give what one will to one's family or particular friends; that is all right. But in a Christmas house-party there is a pleasant interchange of parcels, of which the string and the brown paper and the kindly thought are the really important ingredients, and the gift inside is nothing more than an excuse for those things. . . .

And now I am reminded of the ingenuity of a friend of mine, William by name, who arrived at a large country house for Christmas without any present in his bag. He had expected neither to give nor to receive anything but to his horror he discovered on the twenty-fourth that everybody was preparing a Christmas present for him, and that it was taken for granted that he would require a little privacy and brown paper on Christmas Eve for the purpose of addressing his own offerings to others. He had wild thoughts of telegraphing . . . for something to be sent down, and spoke to other members of the house-party in order to discover what sort of presents would be suitable.

"What are you giving our host?" he asked one of them.

"Mary and I are giving him a book," said John, referring to his wife.

William then approached the youngest son of the house, and discovered that he and his next brother Dick were sharing in this, that, and the other. When he had heard this, William retired to his room and thought profoundly.

He was the first down to breakfast on Christmas morning. All the places at the table were piled high with presents. He looked at John's place. The top parcel said, "To John and Mary from Charles." William took out his fountain-pen and added a couple of words to the inscription. It then read, "To John and Mary from Charles and William," and in William's opinion looked just as effective as before. He moved on to the next place. "To Angela from Father," said the top parcel. "And William," wrote William. At his hostess's place he hesitated for a moment. The first present

there was for "Darling Mother, from her loving children." It did not seem that an "and William" was quite suitable. But his hostess was not to be deprived of William's kindly thought; twenty seconds later the handkerchiefs "from John and Mary and William" expressed all the nice things he was feeling for her. He passed on to the next place. . . .

It is of course impossible to thank every donor of a joint gift; one simply thanks the first person whose eyes one happens to catch. Sometimes William's eye was caught, sometimes not. But he was spared all embarrassment; and I can recommend his solution of the problem with perfect confidence to those who may be in a similar predicament next Christmas.

Christmas
Fun

Jingle Bells

JAMES PIERPONT

1. Dash - ing through the snow in a one - horse o - pen sleigh,
2. A day or two a - go I thought I'd take a ride, And
3. Now the ground is white, go it while you're young,

O'er the fields we go, laugh - ing all the way;
soon Miss Fan - nie Bright was seat - ed by my side; The
Take the girls to - night and sing the sleigh - ing song; Just

Bells on bob - tail ring, mak - ing spir - its bright, What
horse was lean and lank, mis - for - tune seem'd his lot, He
get a bob - tailed nag, two - for - ty for his speed, Then

fun it is to ride and sing a sleigh - ing song to - night!
got in - to a drift - ed bank, and we, we got up - sot. Oh,
hitch him to an o - pen sleigh, and crack! you'll take the lead.

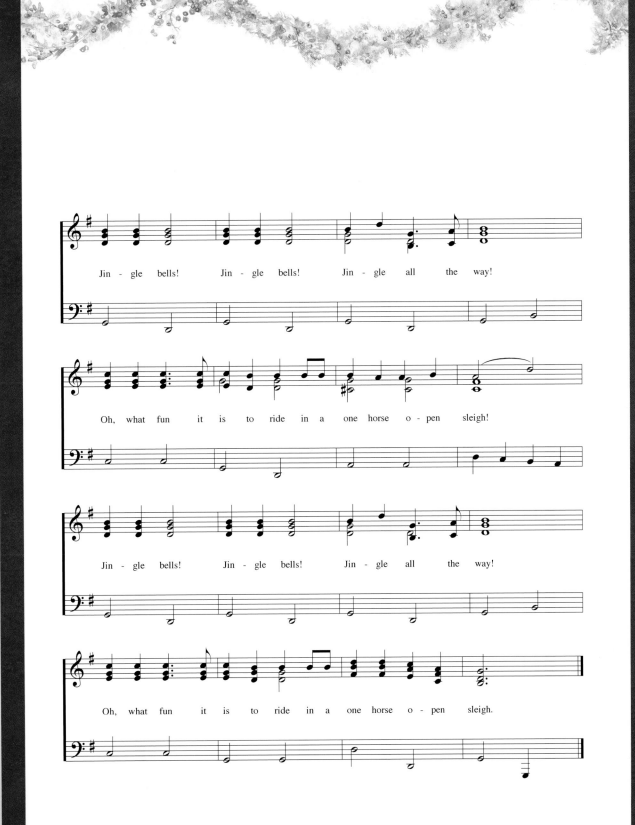

Christmas Fun

The Old-Fashioned Sleigh Ride

Remember the thrill of the old-fashioned sleigh ride,
The straw in the sleigh and the bells ringing clear,
The road stretching white and the moon shining o'er us,
A hand in our own that was clinging and dear?

Remember the thrill of the old-fashioned sleigh ride,
The stretch of the country o'er which we must go,
The meadows so white, and the houses so scattered,
The songs that we sang as we sped through the snow?
"Robin Adarr" and "The Old Oaken Bucket,"
"Tenting Tonight" and "The Sweet By and By."
And all of us sang "When the Roll's Called up Yonder,"
And smiled at the stars in the far-away sky.

Remember the thrill of the old-fashioned sleigh ride,
The lap robes of fur kept us cozy and warm;
The light in the window that beckoned us onward,
The hall when we reached it, its quaintness and charm?
Oh, talk as you like of our modern improvements,
Our autos are nice, and their comfort is plain;
But oh, to be young in the beautiful country,
And ride in an old-fashioned sleigh once again!

ANNE CAMPBELL

Never a Christmas morning
Never the old year ends
But someone thinks of someone
Old says, old times, old friends.

AUTHOR UNKNOWN

Coasting Time

On sleds we coasted down the hill,
Laughing if we took a spill;
We were always glad to know
When the weatherman said snow.

Happy shouts rang on the air
As sleds were gliding everywhere;
Climb the hill, then down you go
Over the white and sparkling snow.

Trudging up the slippery slope,
Pulling sleds by lengths of rope,
When at last we reached the crest,
Pause a while to sit and rest.

Snow and sleds, plus girls and boys,
Gladly welcome winter's joys.

ZELMA BOMAR

Skating

When I try to skate,
My feet are so wary
They grit and they grate;
And then I watch Mary
Easily gliding
Like an ice-fairy,
Skimming and curving,
Out and in,
With a turn of her head
And a lift of her chin
And a gleam of her eye
And a twirl and a spin,
Sailing under
The breathless hush
Of the willows and back
To the frozen rush,
Out to the island
And round the edge,

Skirting the rim
Of the crackling sedge,
Swerving close
To the poplar root
And round the lake
On a single foot,
With a three and an eight
And a loop and a ring;
Where Mary glides,
The lake will sing!
Out in the mist
I hear her now
Under the frost
Of the willow-bough,
Easily sailing,
Light and fleet,
With the song of the lake
Beneath her feet.

HERBERT ASQUITH

Come, Ride with Me to Toyland

Come, ride with me to Toyland,
For this is Christmas Eve,
And just beyond the Dream Road
(Where all is make-believe)
There lies a truly Toyland,
A real and wondrous Joyland,
A little-Girl-and-Boy Land,
Too lovely to conceive!

There Christmas fairies plant a tree
That blossoms forth in stars
And comes to fruit in sugarplums;
There dolls and balls and painted drums

And little trains of cars
All stand and wait for you and me
Beneath the shining wonder-tree.

So saddle up your hobby horse
And ride across the night.
The thundering of our coursers' hoofs
Will put the moon to flight;

And when the east is kitten-gray,
We'll sight that wondrous Joyland;
And at the break of Christmas Day,
We'll gallop into Toyland!

ROWENA BENNETT

My Christmas Sled

BING CROSBY

I can look back over a long list of Christmases. One Christmas above all others stands out in my memory. I was thirteen. We lived in Spokane, Washington, where a white Christmas is standard, and where skating and sledding were the big joys for the youngsters in those days.

Now, if a fella had a "Flexible Flyer" with steel hollow-groove runners, foot rests, and mechanical steering, he could ask the "village belle" to go up to Ledgerwood Hill and spend the day sledding. My eye was on the girl, and my heart was set on the sled. In the few weeks before Christmas, I worked harder than ever at selling newspapers to earn enough money to buy that sled, but I didn't quite make it. I was a few bucks short, but a few bucks in those days came hard. It was a blue Christmas Eve for me that long-ago night in Spokane.

Under the tree for me on Christmas morning was a shiny "Flexible Flyer" with the red, white, and blue eagle on the centerboard. I looked at my dad, my eyes filled with gratitude. "How did you know what I wanted?" I asked. "I have ways," he smiled mysteriously, and as I now know, fathers do. I think my sled was the only "F.F." standing in front of St. Aloysius Church that morning. Afterwards I stood impatiently at the church door with my dad, as he chatted with the priest. I glanced in the direction of the parking area and saw a group of teenagers huddled around the spot where I had put my sled. My heart skipped a beat. I had a horrible thought that one of the cars had run over the sled and that my friends were examining the ruins. I flew down the church steps two at a time. When I reached the group I heard oohs and aahs. There was my sled, just as bright and shiny as ever, and in one whole beautiful piece. I heaved a sigh of relief, contacted my secret love, invited her to go sleigh riding with me, and then we were on our way.

It was a clear crisp December day, and I had the cutest girl and surely the slickest sled on the hill. It was the type of Christmas scene you would expect to see in one of Grandma Moses's paintings. A big bonfire was blazing on the side of the hill. As darkness approached, we spied a coal truck on its way back to town. We flagged it, and then hooked onto that stout rear axle in a long procession of sleds. All the way home we sang, laughed, and pelted one another with snowballs. I have traveled many different "roads" in my motion picture career but that road up Ledgerwood Hill brings to my mind the sweetest memories of all.

Nutcracker Suite Narrative

A little girl marched around her Christmas tree,
And many a marvelous toy had she.
There were cornucopias of sugarplums,
And a mouse with a crown, that sucked its thumbs,
And a fascinating Russian folderol,
Which was a doll inside a doll inside a doll inside a doll,
And a posy as gay as the Christmas lights,
And a picture book of the Arabian nights,
And a painted, silken Chinese fan—
But the one she loved was the nutcracker man.
She thought about him when she went to bed.
With his great long legs and his funny little head.
So she crept downstairs for a last good night,
And arrived in the middle of a furious fight.
The royal mouse that sucked its thumbs
Led an army of mice with swords and drums.
They were battling to seize the toys as slaves
To wait upon them in their secret caves.
The nutcracker man cracked many a crown,
But they overwhelmed him, they whelmed him down,
They were cramming him into a hole in the floor
When the little girl tiptoed to the door.
She had one talent which made her proud,
She could miaow like a cat, and now she miaowed.
A miaow so fierce, a miaow so feline,
That the mice fled home in squealing beeline.
The nutcracker man cracked a hickory nut
To see if his jaws would open and shut,
Then he cracked another and he didn't wince,
And he turned like that into a handsome prince,
And the toys came dancing from the Christmas tree
To celebrate the famous victory.

OGDEN NASH

Christmas Every Day

WILLIAM DEAN HOWELLS

But there is a better thing than the observance of Christmas day, and that is keeping Christmas. —HENRY VAN DYKE

The little girl came into her papa's study, as she always did Saturday morning before breakfast, and asked for a story. He tried to beg off that morning, for he was very busy, but she would not let him. So he began:

"Well, once there was a little pig . . ."

She put her hand over his mouth and stopped him at the word. She said she had heard little pig stories till she was perfectly sick of them.

"Well, what kind of story shall I tell, then?"

"About Christmas. It's getting to be the season. It's past Thanksgiving already."

"It seems to me," argued her papa, "that I've told as often about Christmas as I have about little pigs."

"Christmas is more interesting."

"Well!" Her papa roused himself from his writing by a great effort. "Well, then, I'll tell you about the little girl that wanted Christmas every day in the year. How would you like that?"

"First-rate!" said the little girl; and she nestled into comfortable shape in his lap, ready for listening.

"Very well, then, this little pig—Oh, what are you pounding me for?"

"Because you said little pig instead of little girl."

"I should like to know what's the difference between a little pig and a little girl that wanted it Christmas every day!"

"Papa," said the little girl, warningly, "if you don't go on, I'll give it to you!" And at this her papa darted off like lightning, and began to tell the story as fast as he could.

Well, once there was a little girl who liked Christmas so much that she wanted it to be Christmas every day in the year; and as soon as Thanksgiving was over she began to send postal cards to the old Christmas Fairy to ask if she mightn't have it. But the old Fairy never answered any of the postals; and, after a while, the little girl found out that the Fairy was pretty particular, and wouldn't even notice anything but

letters, not even correspondence cards in envelopes; but real letters on sheets of paper, and sealed outside with a monogram—or your initial, any way. So, then, she began to send her letters; and in about three weeks—or just the day before Christmas, it was—she got a letter from the Fairy, saying she might have it Christmas every day for a year, and then they would see about having it longer.

The little girl was a good deal excited already, preparing for the old-fashioned, once-a-year Christmas that was coming the next day, and perhaps the Fairy's promise didn't make such an impression on her as it would have made at some other time. She just resolved to keep it to herself, and surprise everybody with it as it kept coming true; and then it slipped out of her mind altogether.

She had a splendid Christmas. She went to bed early, so as to let Santa Claus have a chance at the stockings, and in the morning she was up the first of anybody and went and felt them, and found hers all lumpy with packages of candy, and oranges and grapes, and pocket-books and rubber balls and all kinds of small presents, and her big brother's with nothing but the tongs in them, and her young lady sister's with a new silk umbrella, and her papa's and mamma's with potatoes and pieces of coal wrapped up in tissue paper, just as they always had every Christmas. Then she waited around till the rest of the family were up, and she was the first to burst into the library, when the doors were opened, and look at the large presents laid out on the library-table—books, and portfolios, and boxes of stationery, and breast-pins, and dolls, and little stoves, and dozens of handkerchiefs, and ink-stands, and skates, and snow-shovels, and photograph frames, and little easels, and boxes of watercolors, and Turkish paste, and nougat, and candied cherries, and dolls' houses, and waterproofs—and the big Christmas tree, lighted and standing in a waste-basket in the middle.

She had a splendid Christmas all day. She ate so much candy that she did not want any breakfast; and the whole forenoon the presents kept pouring in that the expressman had not had time to deliver the night before; and she went 'round giving the presents she had got for other people, and came home and ate turkey and cranberry for dinner, and plum-pudding and nuts and raisins and oranges and more candy, and then went out and coasted and came in with a stomach-ache, crying; and her papa said he would see if his house was turned into that sort of fool's paradise another year; and they had a light supper, and pretty early everybody went to bed cross.

Here the little girl pounded her papa in the back, again.

"Well, what now? Did I say pigs?"

"You made them act like pigs."

"Well, didn't they?"

"No matter; you oughtn't to put it into a story."

"Very well, then, I'll take it all out."

Her father went on:

The little girl slept very heavily, and she slept very late, but she was wakened at last by the other children dancing 'round her bed with their stockings full of presents in their hands.

"What is it?" said the little girl, and she rubbed her eyes and tried to rise up in bed.

"Christmas! Christmas! Christmas!" they all shouted, and waved their stockings.

"Nonsense! It was Christmas yesterday."

Her brothers and sisters just laughed. "We don't know about that. It's Christmas to-day, any way. You come into the library and see."

Then all at once it flashed on the little girl that the Fairy was keeping her promise, and her year of Christmases was beginning. She was dreadfully sleepy, but she sprang up like a lark—a lark that had overeaten itself and gone to bed cross—and darted into the library. There it was again! Books, and portfolios, and boxes of stationery, and breast-pins—

"You needn't go over it all, Papa; I guess I can remember just what was there," said the little girl.

There was the Christmas tree blazing away, and the family picking out their presents, and her father perfectly puzzled, and her mother ready to cry. "I'm sure I don't see how I'm to dispose of all these things," said her mother, and her father said it seemed to him they had had something just like it the day before, but he supposed he must have dreamed it. This struck the little girl as the best kind of joke; and so she ate so much candy she didn't want any breakfast, and went 'round carrying presents, and had turkey and cranberry for dinner, and then went out and coasted, and came in with a—

"Papa!"

"Well, what now?"

"What did you promise, you forgetful thing?"

"Oh! oh, yes!"

Well, the next day, it was just the same thing over again, but everybody getting crosser; and at the end of a week's time so many people had lost their tempers that you could pick up lost tempers everywhere; they perfectly strewed the ground. Even when people tried to recover their tempers they usually got somebody else's, and it made the most dreadful mix.

The little girl began to get frightened, keeping the secret all to herself; she wanted to tell her mother, but she didn't dare to; and she was ashamed to ask the Fairy to take back her gift, it seemed ungrateful and ill-bred, and she thought she would try to stand it, but she hardly knew how she could, for a whole year. So it went on and on, and it was Christmas on St. Valentine's Day and Washington's Birthday just the same as any day, and it didn't skip even the First of April, though everything was counterfeit that day, and that was some little relief.

After a while, coal and potatoes began to be awfully scarce, so many had been wrapped up in tissue paper to fool papas and mammas with. Turkeys got to be about a thousand dollars apiece—

"Papa!"

"Well, what?"

"You're beginning to fib."

"Well, two thousand, then."

And they got to passing off almost anything for turkeys—half-grown hummingbirds, and even rocs out of the "Arabian Nights"—the real turkeys were so scarce. And cranberries—well, they asked a diamond apiece for cranberries. All the woods and orchards were cut down for Christmas trees, and where the woods and orchards used to be, it looked just like a stubble-field with the stumps. After a while they had to make Christmas trees out of rags and stuff them with bran, like old-fashioned dolls; but there were plenty of rags because people got so poor, buying presents for one another, that they couldn't get any new clothes, and they just wore their old ones to tatters. They got so poor that everybody had to go to the poor-house, except the confectioners, and the fancy store-keepers, and the picture booksellers, and the expressmen; and they all got so rich and proud that they would hardly wait upon a person when he came to buy; it was perfectly shameful!

After it had gone on about three or four months, the little girl, whenever she came into the room in the morning and saw those great ugly lumpy stockings dangling at the fireplace and the disgusting presents around everywhere, used to just sit down and burst out crying. In six months she was perfectly exhausted; she couldn't even cry any more; she just lay on the lounge and rolled her eyes and panted. About the beginning of October she took to sitting down on dolls wherever she found them—French dolls or any kind—she hated the sight of them so; and by Thanksgiving she was crazy, and just slammed her presents across the room.

By that time people didn't carry presents around nicely any more. They flung them over the fence or through the window or anything; and instead of running their tongues out and taking great pains to write "For dear Papa," or "Mamma," or "Brother," or "Sister," or "Susie," or "Sammie," or "Billie," or "Bobby," or "Jimmie," or "Jennie," or whoever it was, and troubling to get the spelling right, and then signing their names, and "Xmas 188-," they used to write in the gift-books, "Take it, you horrid old thing!" and then go and bang it against the front door. Nearly everybody had built barns to hold their presents, but pretty soon the barns overflowed, and then they used to let them lie out in the rain or anywhere. Sometimes the police used to come and tell them to shovel their presents off the sidewalk, or they would arrest them. Did I tell you how it was on the Fourth of July?

"No, how was it?" And the little girl nestled closer, in expectation of something uncommon.

Well, the night before, the boys stayed up to celebrate, as they always do, and fell asleep before twelve o'clock, as usual, expecting to be wakened by the bells and cannon. But it was nearly eight o'clock before the first boy in the United States woke up, and then he found out what the trouble was. As soon as he could get his clothes on, he ran out of the house and smashed a big cannon-torpedo down on the pavement; but it didn't make any more noise than a damp wad of paper, and, after he tried about twenty or thirty more, he began to pick them up and look at them. Every single torpedo was a big raisin! Then he just streaked it upstairs and examined his firecrackers and toy-pistol and two-dollar collection of fireworks and found that they were nothing but sugar and candy painted up to look like fireworks! Before ten o'clock, every boy in the United States found out that his Fourth of July things had turned into Christmas things; and then they just sat down and cried—they were so mad. The Fourth of July orations all turned into Christmas carols, and when anybody tried to read the Declaration, instead of saying, "When in the course of human events it becomes necessary," he was sure to sing, "God rest you, merry gentlemen." It was perfectly awful.

The little girl drew a deep sigh of satisfaction. "And how was it at Thanksgiving?" she asked.

Her papa hesitated. "Well, I'm almost afraid to tell you. I'm afraid you'll think it's wicked."

"Well, tell, anyway," said the little girl.

Well, before it came Thanksgiving, it had leaked out who had caused all these Christmases. The little girl had suffered so much that she had talked about it in her sleep; and after that, hardly anybody would play with her. People just perfectly despised her because, if it had not been for her greediness, it wouldn't have happened; and now, when it came Thanksgiving, and she wanted them to go to church and have a squash-pie and turkey and show their gratitude, they said that all the turkeys had been eaten up for her old Christmas dinners, and if she would stop the Christmases, they would see about the gratitude.

Wasn't it dreadful? And the very next day the little girl began to send letters to the Christmas Fairy, and then telegrams, to stop it. But it didn't do any good; and then she got to calling at the Fairy's house, but the girl that came to the door always said "Not at home," or "Engaged" or "At dinner" or something like that; and so it went on till it came to the old once-a-year Christmas Eve. The little girl fell asleep, and when she woke up in the morning—

"She found it was all nothing but a dream," suggested the little girl.

"No, indeed!" said her papa. "It was all every bit true!"

"Well, what did she find out then?"

"Why, that it wasn't Christmas at last, and wasn't ever going to be, any more. Now it's time for breakfast."

The little girl held her papa fast around the neck.

"You shan't go if you're going to leave it so!"

"How do you want it left?"

"Christmas once a year."

"All right," said her papa; and he went on again.

Well, there was the greatest rejoicing all over the country, and it extended clear up into Canada. The people met together everywhere and kissed and cried for joy. The city carts went around and gathered up all the candy and raisins and nuts, and dumped them into the river; and it made the fish perfectly sick; and the whole United States, as far out as Alaska, was one blaze of bonfires, where the children were burning up their gift-books and presents of all kinds. They had the greatest time!

The little girl went to thank the old Fairy because she had stopped it being Christmas, and she said she hoped she would keep her promise and see that Christmas never, never came again. Then the Fairy frowned, and asked her if she was sure she knew what she meant; and the little girl asked her, why not? and the old Fairy said that now she was behaving just as greedily as ever, and she'd better look out. This made the little girl think it all over carefully again, and she said she would be willing to have it Christmas about once in a thousand years and then she said a hundred, and then she said ten, and at last she got down to one. Then the Fairy said that was the good old way that had pleased people ever since Christmas began, and she was agreed. Then the little girl said, "What're your shoes made of?" And the Fairy said, "Leather." And the little girl said, "Bargain's done forever," and skipped off, and hippity-hopped the whole way home, she was so glad.

"How will that do?" asked the papa.

"First-rate!" said the little girl; but she hated to have the story stop and was rather sober. However, her mamma put her head in at the door and asked her papa:

"Are you never coming to breakfast? What have you been telling that child?"

"Oh, just a moral tale."

The little girl caught him around the neck again.

"We know! Don't you tell what, Papa! Don't you tell what!"

Christmas Joy

Christmas Joy

Somehow, not only for Christmas
But all the long year through,
The joy that you give to others
Is the joy that comes back to you.

JOHN GREENLEAF WHITTIER

Merry Christmas

I saw on the snow
when I tried my skis
the track of a mouse
beside some trees.

Before he tunneled
to reach his house
he wrote "Merry Christmas"
in white, in mouse.

AILEEN FISHER

Angels in the Snow

We used to play in winter's snow
By making angel wings you know.
We'd lie so still with arms up high,
In snow that was so smooth and dry.

Then through the snow, all white and deep,
Our arms so carefully we sweep
Until our hands o'erhead we bring;
Each arm has made an angel's wing.

Then up we rise with greatest care,
Not to disturb the images there,
And gaze with wonder at the row
Of Christmas angels in the snow.

IRMA SANBORN

Snowflakes

And did you know
That every flake of snow
That forms so high
In the grey winter sky
And falls so far,
Is a bright six-pointed star?
Each crystal grows
A flower as perfect as a rose.
Lace could never make
The patterns of a flake.
No brooch
Of figured silver could approach
Its delicate craftsmanship. And think:
Each pattern is distinct.
Of all the snowflakes floating there—
The million million in the air—
None is the same. Each star
Is newly forged, as faces are,
Shaped to its own design
Like yours and mine.
And yet . . . each one
Melts when its flight is done;
Holds frozen loveliness
A moment, even less;
Suspends itself in time—
And passes like a rhyme.

CLIVE SANSOM

The Children's Carol

Here we come again, again, and here we come again!
Christmas is a single pearl swinging on a chain,
Christmas is a single flower in a barren wood,
Christmas is a single sail on the salty flood,
Christmas is a single star in the empty sky,
Christmas is a single song sung for charity,
Here we come again, again, to sing to you again,
Give a single penny that we may not sing in vain.

ELEANOR FARJEON

Once There Was a Snowman

Once there was a snowman
    Who stood outside the door.
He wished that he could come inside
    And run about the floor.
He wished that he could warm himself
    Beside the fire, so red.
He wished that he could climb
    Upon the big white bed.

So he called to the North Wind,
    "Come and help me, pray,
For I'm completely frozen
    Standing out here all day."
So the North Wind came along
    And blew him in the door,
And now there's nothing left of him
    But a puddle on the floor!

AUTHOR UNKNOWN

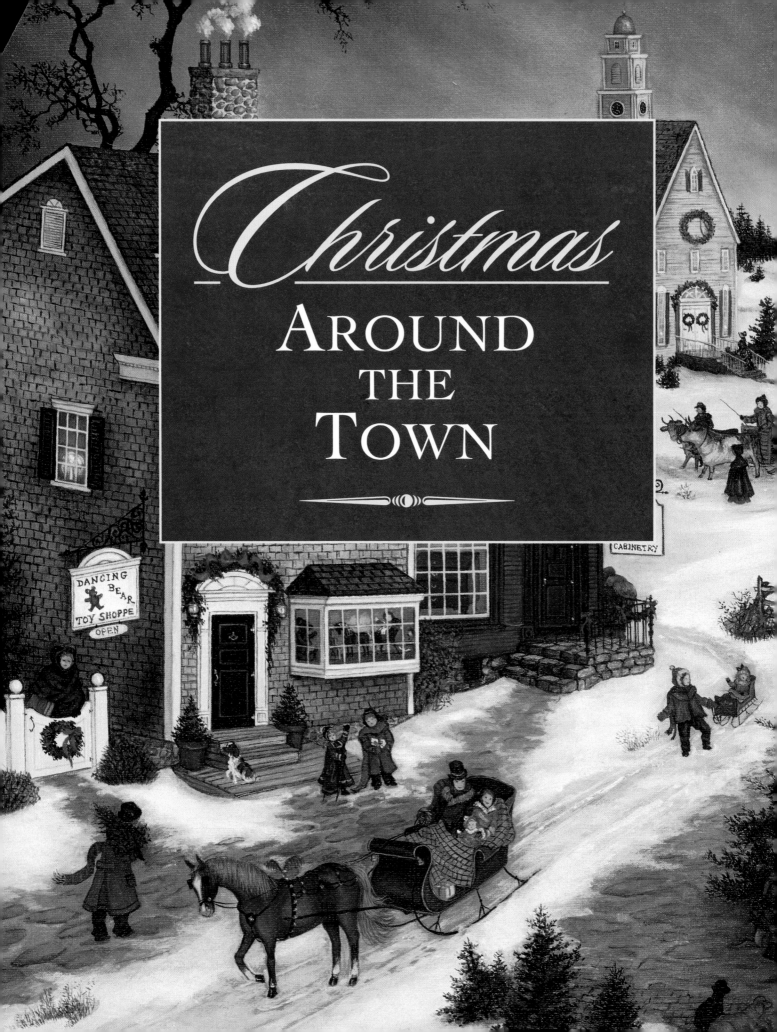

Christmas
Around the Town

O Come, All Ye Faithful

Translated by Canon Frederick Oakeley

J. F. Wade

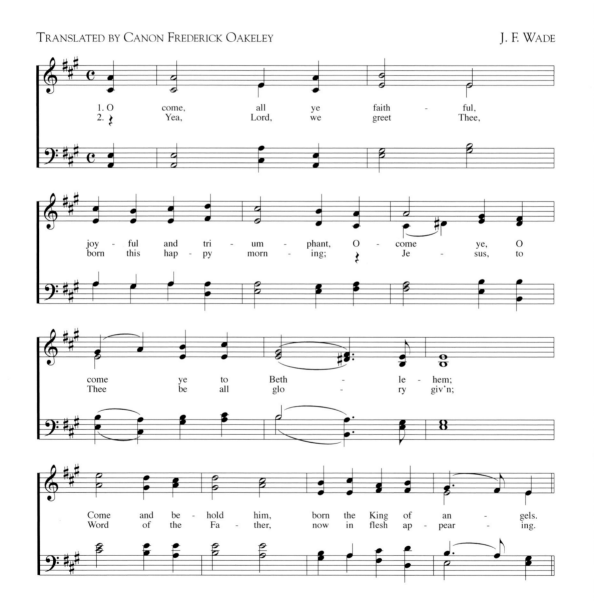

A Christmas Spectacle

ROBERT BENCHLEY

Let's dance and sing and make good cheer,
for Christmas comes but once a year.
—GEORGE MACFERRAN

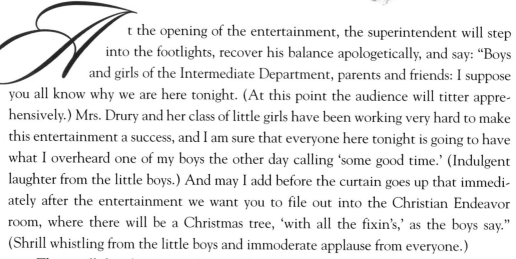

At the opening of the entertainment, the superintendent will step into the footlights, recover his balance apologetically, and say: "Boys and girls of the Intermediate Department, parents and friends: I suppose you all know why we are here tonight. (At this point the audience will titter apprehensively.) Mrs. Drury and her class of little girls have been working very hard to make this entertainment a success, and I am sure that everyone here tonight is going to have what I overheard one of my boys the other day calling 'some good time.' (Indulgent laughter from the little boys.) And may I add before the curtain goes up that immediately after the entertainment we want you to file out into the Christian Endeavor room, where there will be a Christmas tree, 'with all the fixin's,' as the boys say." (Shrill whistling from the little boys and immoderate applause from everyone.)

There will then be a wait of twenty-five minutes, while sounds of hammering and dropping may be heard from behind the curtains. The Boys Club orchestra will render the "Poet and Peasant Overture" four times in succession, each time differently.

At last one side of the curtains will be drawn back; the other will catch on something and have to be released by hand; someone will whisper loudly, "Put out the lights," following which the entire house will be plunged into darkness. Amid catcalls from the little boys, the spotlights will at last go on, disclosing the windows in the rear of the vestry, rather ineffectively concealed by a group of small fir trees on standards, one of which has already fallen over, leaving exposed a corner of the map of Palestine and the list of gold-star classes for November. In the center of the stage is a larger tree, undecorated.

Twenty-five seconds too early, little Flora Rochester will prance out from the wings, uttering the first shrill notes of a song, and will have to be grabbed by eager hands and pulled back. Twenty-four seconds later the piano will begin "The Return of the Reindeer" with a powerful accent on the first note of each bar, and Flora Rochester, Lillian McNulty, Gertrude Hamingham, and Martha Wrist will swirl on, dressed in white, and advance heavily into the footlights, which will go out.

There will then be an interlude while Mr. Neff, the sexton, adjusts the connection, during which the four little girls stand undecided whether to brave it out or cry. As a compromise they giggle and are herded back into the wings by Mrs. Drury amid applause. When the lights go on again, the applause becomes deafening, and as Mr. Neff walks triumphantly away, the little boys in the audience will whistle: "There she goes, there she goes, all dressed up in her Sunday clothes!"

"The Return of the Reindeer" will be started again and the showgirls will reappear, this time more gingerly and somewhat dispirited. They will, however, sing the following, to the music of the "Ballet Pizzicato" from "Sylvia":

> We greet you, we greet you,
> On this Christmas Eve so fine.
> We greet you, we greet you,
> And wish you a good time.

They will then turn toward the tree and Flora Rochester will advance, hanging a silver star on one of the branches, meanwhile reciting a verse, the only distinguishable words of which are: "I am Faith so strong and pure. . . ." At the conclusion of her recitation, the star will fall off.

Lillian McNulty will then step forward and hang her star on a branch, reading her lines in clear tones:

> And I am Hope, a virtue great,
> My gift to Christmas now I make,
> That children and grown-ups may hope today
> That tomorrow will be a merry Christmas Day.

The hanging of the third star will be consummated by Gertrude Hamingham, who will get as far as "Sweet Charity I bring to place upon the tree . . ." at which point the strain will become too great, and she will forget the remainder. After several frantic glances toward the wings, from which Mrs. Drury is sending out whispered messages to the effect that the next line begins, "My message bright . . ."

Gertrude will disappear, crying softly.

After the morale of the cast has been in some measure restored by the pianist, who, with great presence of mind, plays a few bars of "Will There Be Any Stars in My Crown?" to cover up Gertrude's exit, Martha Wrist will unleash a rope of silver tinsel from the foot of the tree and, stringing it over the boughs as she skips around in a circle, will say, with great assurance:

> Round and round the tree I go,
> Through the holly and the snow
> Bringing love and Christmas cheer
> Through the happy year to come.

At this point there will be a great commotion and the jangling of sleighbells off-stage; and Mr. Creamer, rather poorly disguised as Santa Claus, will emerge. A great popular demonstration for Mr. Creamer will follow. He will then advance to the footlights and, rubbing his pillow to denote joviality, will say thickly through his false beard: "Well, well, well, what have we here? A lot of bad little boys and girls who aren't going to get any Christmas presents this year? (Nervous laughter from the little boys and girls.) Let me see, let me see! I have a note here from Dr. Whidden. Let's see what it says. (Reads from a paper on which there is obviously nothing written.) 'If you and the young people of the Intermediate Department will come into the Christian Endeavor room, I think we may have a little surprise for you.' Well, well, well! What do you suppose it can be? (Cries of "I know, I know!" from sophisticated ones in the audience.) Well, anyway, suppose we go out and see? Now if Miss Liftnagle will oblige us with a little march on the piano, we will all form in single file."

At this point there will ensue a stampede toward the Christian Endeavor room, in which chairs will be broken, decorations demolished, and the protesting Mr. Creamer badly hurt.

This will bring to a close the first part of the entertainment.

In Dulci Jubilo: A Table for Carolers

JANE GRIGSON

*Be merry all! Be merry all! With holly dress
the festival hall; prepare the song, the feast, the ball
to welcome Merry Christmas.*—W. R. SPENCER

One of my earliest memories is of my father singing at Christmas. *Adeste,
fideles, Laeti triumphantes.* He had a lovely tenor voice, clear, unaffected,
warm, and joyful. It burst from him, escaping his local-government-official
envelope of striped gray trousers, black coat, even spats when I was very young, with
a vigor that makes me wonder what emotions were held back, deep inside, by the dam
of his normal disciplined behavior. He is ninety-one now and cannot sing anymore,
but I still lack the nerve to probe this particular mystery.

He sang loudly in his cold bath. He sang at the weekends, taught us songs, while
our mother played the piano. Above all he sang at matins when we formed a demure,
tidy row in church, about twelve pews back from the choir. Nobody else in the congregation sang very much. They were too refined. He didn't care. I suspect he didn't
notice, but if we were silent, he would glance at us in a pained way, wondering if perhaps we might be coming down with something. As a young man he had sung in
church choirs and knew how to stress the psalms as they were chanted. "My heart is
inditing of a good matter . . . Full of grace are thy lips . . . My tongue is the pen of a
ready writer . . . O praise God in His holiness, praise Him in the firmament of His
power . . . Let everything that hath breath prai-ai-ai-aise the Lord!" And, come
Christmas, he taught us how to pronounce choral Latin: "*In dulci jubilo,* Now sing we
all *Io, Io* . . . Our heart's joy reclineth *In praesepio!*" emerged from our infant throats
without stumble or inaccuracy.

Looking back now, I see that the greatest gift he gave me was not the rules for a
good life so sweetly and earnestly instilled, but the unconscious acceptance that
music and poetry, especially in combination, are the greatest of man's achievements.
At every season, in every event that marks my life, that feeling is there. Words and
music well up, comfort, companionship, pain, and delight.

And so it is that we have always begun our Christmas, in my father's way—with carol singing, which by a strange coincidence, for his character was very different, happened to be my husband's way too. Our Christmas bears no relation to the old rollicking festivities of the distant past, and not even a very close relationship to the Christmas that was invented in Britain by the Victorians. We ignore the pandemonium of the shops until the last few days. Christmas tree, wreath for the front door, decorations never make an appearance until three o'clock on Christmas Eve. We switch on the radio and wait in a tense hush for that first pure note of the boy's voice, "Once in Royal David's City," from King's College chapel.

My father was at Cambridge. So was I. So were all of my husband Geoffrey's family from the sixteenth century to his generation, when he and his brothers went to Oxford and broke the rule. As the choir comes nearer and we hear the red and white robes swishing gently to the sound, we are glad to be busy. That way we can disguise our tears as the Chaplain reads the Bidding Prayer, reminding us of those who rejoice in a greater light and on a farther shore, whose multitude no man can number, with whom we ever more are one. In that language, in that music

we do confer with who are gone,
And the dead living unto counsel call:

and by that language, that music, we know

th' unborn shall have communion
Of what we feel, and what doth us befall.

That is Christmas, our own private but universal start.

Christmas Caroling

Caroling

There's no sweeter sound
Than carols sung
By a group of voices
Clear and young.
Akin to the angels
Of long ago,
The notes float out
O'er the glistening snow.

And as the voices
Rise and blend,
The listener hopes
It shall never end
This way of telling
A waiting earth,
The age-old news
Of a Saviour's birth.

VIRGINIA BLANCK MOORE

The Carolers

Under my window the carolers sang
Songs loved at Christmastime;
Clear, through the darkness, child voices rang,
Singing, "O Holy Night."

Out of my mind fled the worry and care
Left from the day's swift pace;
Under my window, in half-light there
I glimpsed an infant face.

Gazing, amazed at the star-studded sky
And at the rosy light
Bathing the wreath in my window high . . .
Truly a lovely sight!

Under my window wee carolers bold
Sang, enthralling me quite.
Surely this night, like that night of old,
Is a most holy night!

EDWARD E. BILL

Carols to a Neighbor

As long as a friendly light
Glows out your windowpane,
A soft petition into night,
Another carol we will sing to you,
A Christmas Eve refrain.

As long as one candle burns
From out your windowsill,
Through spatterfrost and ferns,
Another carol we will sing to you
Of peace and God's goodwill.

As long as we can see a star,
Radiant on your Christmas tree,
Spreading love and welcome far,
Another carol we will sing to you:
A promised child's Nativity.

As long as a single lamp
Shows eagerness through windowframe,
Of Magi march and shepherd tramp,
Another carol we will sing to you,
And hymn His blessed name.

MAURICE W. FOGLE

Here We Come A-Caroling

Here we come a-caroling
Among the leaves so green;
Here we come a-wand'ring
So fair to be seen.

Love and joy come to you,
And to you glad Christmas too,
And God bless you and send you a Happy New Year,
And God send you a Happy New Year.

Bless the master of this house,
Likewise the mistress too,
And we the little children that 'round the table go.

Love and joy come to you,
And to you glad Christmas too,
And God bless you and send you a Happy New Year,
And God send you a Happy New Year.

AUTHOR UNKNOWN

Carol

Villagers all, this frosty tide,
Let your doors swing open wide,
Though wind may follow, and snow beside,
Yet draw us in by your fire to bide;
    Joy shall be yours in the morning!

Here we stand in the cold and the sleet,
Blowing fingers and stamping feet,
Come from far away you to greet—
You by the fire and we in the street—
    Bidding you joy in the morning!

KENNETH GRAHAME

The Loving Gift

GLORIA A. TRUITT

The joy of brightening other lives, supplanting empty hearts and lives with generous gifts becomes for us the magic of Christmas. —W. C. JONES

Mother watched Laura carry the box of freshly baked cookies across the street to Mrs. Gilly's door. She turned to give her mother a brave smile, and then pressed the doorbell. Laura wished her stomach would stop doing flip-flops. She had not wanted to deliver the cookies because she had never talked with Mrs. Gilly. She was afraid she wouldn't know what to say. Soon the door opened and Laura disappeared into Mrs. Gilly's front hall.

An hour later, Laura's mother looked at the kitchen clock. It was suppertime and Laura still wasn't home. When she heard Laura's father coming home, she decided not to wait any longer. Just as she picked up the phone to call, Laura ran into the house. "Mother! Mother!" Laura called excitedly. "I had the best time with Mrs. Gilly! You should see her doll collection!"

During supper, Laura told her mother and father about Mrs. Gilly. "Mrs. Gilly told me all about her life," said Laura. "It was such an exciting story, I forgot about the time."

"I understand," said mother. "Will you tell us about her dolls?"

"Oh, they're just wonderful," sighed Laura. "Mrs. Gilly is eighty-six years old, and some of the dolls are almost as old as she is! She keeps them on shelves in a big, glass case, and there's a story about each one of them!"

At bedtime, Laura asked her mother if she could visit Mrs. Gilly again. "She's very old," said Laura thoughtfully, "and I think she's lonely."

Time passed and Laura's visits to Mrs. Gilly became quite regular. Three afternoons a week she stopped by to chat with her new-found friend, and each time she came home with an interesting story to tell her mother.

Laura told mother about the lovely doll with the China head and a very strange doll that was made from corncob. "The oldest doll still wears its original dress!" exclaimed Laura. "It was made by Mrs. Gilly's mother—and it doesn't have a single tear in it—can you imagine that?"

Mother smiled and said, "I'm sure they are all beautiful, Laura, and I'm glad Mrs. Gilly has time to tell you about them."

"You know, Mother, they are all beautiful, but the most beautiful doll of all is not very big or old, compared to the rest. It's a black-haired doll with a pink gown and matching hat. Mrs. Gilly's sister made the doll, and gave it to her on her sixty-fifth birthday!"

One Saturday morning, Laura woke up to find the ground covered with snow. She bounced out of bed when she remembered that this was the day her father had promised to get their Christmas tree. After breakfast the family went to the tree farm where they inspected hundreds of trees. Finally they decided on a beautiful Norway spruce. As her father tied it to the top of the car, Laura slowly walked over to a small, but perfectly shaped balsam fir. "Oh, please, could we get this one for Mrs. Gilly?" called Laura. "It would be just perfect for her!"

"That's a wonderful idea," said father. When the family arrived home, mother and father helped Laura carry the tree to Mrs. Gilly's house. When Mrs. Gilly saw the pretty balsam fir, her eyes filled with tears of happiness. "How can I thank you?" she asked, hugging Laura tightly.

"You don't have to," answered Laura, "you're my friend—and this is a special time for love."

"You're right, Laura," said Mrs. Gilly, "Christmas is the time to celebrate the greatest gift of love—the birth of Jesus."

After they had visited for a while, Mother said it was time to go. Just as Laura was going out through the door, Mrs. Gilly said, "Wait a minute, Laura. I almost forgot to give you something."

Quickly, Mrs. Gilly picked up a brown paper bag

from the table and tucked it under Laura's arm. "It's a small gift," said Mrs. Gilly, "but I'd like you to have it as a keepsake."

At once Laura knew what was in the bag because the tiny doll in the pink gown was no longer standing in the glass case. Laura hugged Mrs. Gilly and said "Thank you" over and over again. Then everyone laughed happily as Laura took the little doll from the bag and cried, "This isn't a small gift, Mrs. Gilly! It—it's the biggest love gift I've ever had! Thank you, thank you, thank you!"

The Lesser Christmas Miracle

JULIE MCDONALD

Christmas is real to us only if we have a heart that holds the heart of Christmas. —ESTHER BALDWIN YORK

It's easy for an Iowa child to believe what my Danish grandmother told me—that the farm animals celebrate the birth of Christ with human utterance at midnight on Christmas Eve. I first believed it on a farm near Fiscus, and it flowed like a sweet undercurrent beneath the many preparations for the holidays.

A piece had to be learned for the Christmas program at Merrill's Grove Baptist Church, and I was admonished not to twist the hem of my skirt to immodest heights while delivering it. I performed without a lapse of memory and left my hemline alone; and when the program was over, we all got brown paper bags filled with hard candy. The bumpy raspberries with soft centers were my favorites, but I also admired the small rounds with a flower that remained visible until the candy was sucked to a sliver.

I had plans to visit the barn at midnight to hear what the cattle had to say to each other; but I kept them to myself, sensing that I would be thwarted should anyone find out. The paradoxically soft and stark light of the kerosene lamps shone on the clock face I could not yet read, and I asked again and again, "Is it midnight yet?" I had never experienced a midnight, and that prospect plus talking animals was almost too much excitement to bear.

My parents spoke of Santa Claus, which presented a problem. If I went to the barn at midnight to listen to the animals, Santa Claus would have to wait to bring my presents, and he might not be able to work me into his route. What to do?

Exhaustion solved my dilemma. I awoke in my own bed in the cold light of Christmas morning and hurried to the dining room to see what Santa had brought with no more than a fleeting regret about missing the animal conversation. There would be other years, other midnights. Now there was the joy of a small table painted bright orange and a sack of peanuts in the shell. The gifts seemed wonderful to me, and I had no notion of the thought and struggle that went into them in that Depression year. For years I did not know that my father made the table from an apple box, a broomstick, and the core of a linoleum roll or that finding a few cents to buy peanuts involved looking through pockets and old purses for forgotten coins.

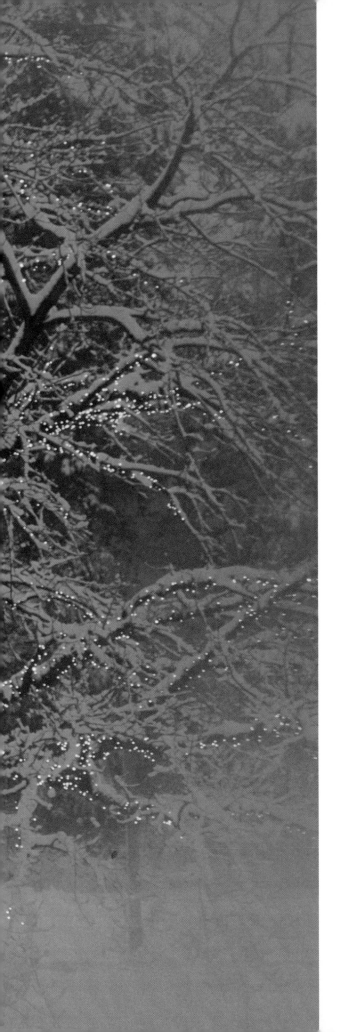

Later in the morning I went to the barn, hoping that the cattle still might have the power to speak, but they didn't. I had missed the moment, and now they only chewed and exhaled their grain-sweet breath in my face. "I'll come next year," I said, but I never did. That was my last Christmas on the farm and my father's last Christmas on earth. We moved to town.

In Harlan, Christmas meant colored lights strung from the Shelby County courthouse like a brilliant spider web, blue electric candles in Aunt Mary's window, and in Grandma's house (where we were living), a Christmas tree with wax candles, so lovely and so dangerous. We walked the streets of the town and admired the electric lights in other peoples' windows.

There were other Christmases in other houses; and for our family, hard times persisted, but they didn't seem so hard at the time. One year when we couldn't afford a Christmas tree, we cut a bough from the huge pine on the family cemetery plot and thrust it into a crock of sand. Then we punctured our fingers stringing popcorn and cranberries and made chains of paper loops to decorate it. The bough smelled as a Christmas tree should, but it also wept resin, recalling its funereal origin. That crying "tree" was banked with the best gifts we could manage, and I recall my delight with a glamorous milk glass flower pot filled with bath salts topped by a shiny and unnatural blue poinsettia.

In town, I could not go to the barn to listen to the animals talking, but I thought of them and wondered what they would say.

Many years later when I had children of my own, we were house-sitting for my in-laws in Davenport at Christmas, and I was the last one up, filling stockings. As midnight struck with Westminster chimes, I considered going to the stable. I even reached for my coat, but I hung it up again. Mute horses would have stolen something precious from me. This dearest Christmas fancy of an Iowa child was something I wanted to keep, and I have. Surely the miraculous reason for Christmas can support this endearing lesser miracle.

Christmas Treats

Season's Greetings

The season's at its merriest,
Excitement's in the air.
The turkey's bought and gifts are brought
From almost everywhere.

I've mailed a lot of Christmas cards
To send a wish of cheer;
They never say it quite the way
I'd speak if you were here.

My wish for you at Christmastime
Is based on hours of thought . . .
I hope it brings you greater things
Than gifts I might have bought.

Just look and see your Christmas tree
For what it means again,
As a little child might see it
From outside your windowpane.

May the food upon your table
Be enough, with some to share.
And may it treat you warm and sweet
As your mother's blessing prayer.

May you have ears this Christmastime
To hear the joyous bells,
And choirs repeat the music sweet
That such a story tells.

I wish for you the eyes to see
The wealth of little things
That softly beam beneath the gleam
This season also brings.

But, most of all, I wish for you
A season bright and gay.
May you recall above it all
That other Christmas Day.

ALICE L. MASON

Hot Mulled Cider

8	cups apple cider or juice	1	teaspoon whole allspice
½	cup packed light brown sugar	1	teaspoon whole cloves
6	sticks of cinnamon	8	thin orange slices
1	teaspoon nutmeg		

In a large pan, combine apple cider, brown sugar, and nutmeg. In a cheesecloth, combine cinnamon, allspice, and cloves; tie and add to cider. Bring to a boil. Reduce heat, cover, and simmer 10 minutes. Remove bag. Serve cider in mugs garnished with an orange slice. Makes 8 one-cup servings.

Glazed Nuts

1½	cups blanched whole almonds, cashews, or pecan halves	½	cup granulated sugar
		1	tablespoon butter

Butter a baking sheet or large sheet of aluminum foil and set aside. In a heavy 8-inch skillet, combine nuts, sugar, and butter. Cook over medium heat, stirring constantly, for 6 to 8 minutes or until sugar turns golden brown and nuts are toasted. Spread nuts on the foil, separating into clusters. Sprinkle lightly with salt. Makes ½ pound.

Hot Spiced Chocolate

1	cup water	1	teaspoon ground cinnamon
2	squares (2 oz.) unsweetened chocolate	¼	teaspoon ground nutmeg
⅓	cup granulated sugar	4	cups milk
	Dash salt		Whipped cream

In a large saucepan, combine water, chocolate, sugar, and salt. Stir over medium-low heat just until chocolate melts. Stir in cinnamon and nutmeg. Gradually stir in milk; heat just to a boil but *do not boil*. Remove from heat and serve in warm mugs. Top each serving with a dollop of whipped cream and a sprinkling of cinnamon. Makes 4 one-cup servings.

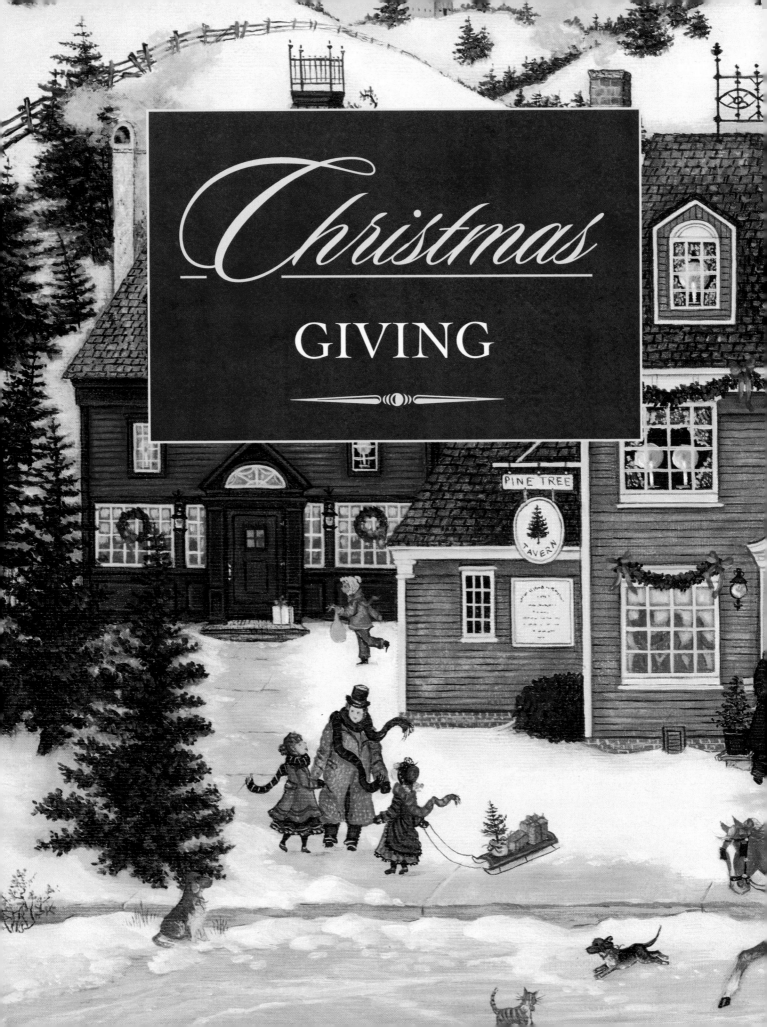

Christmas
GIVING

The Little Drummer Boy

KATHERINE DAVIS, HENRY ONORATI,
AND HARRY SIMEONE

rum - pum - pum - pum, rum - pum - pum - pum, rum - pum - pum - pum)
rum - pum - pum - pum, rum - pum - pum - pum, rum - pum - pum - pum)
rum - pum - pum - pum, rum - pum - pum - pum, rum - pum - pum - pum)

So   to   hon - or Him   (Pa -
Shall   I   play   for You   (Pa -
Then   He   smiled at   me,   (Pa -

rum - pum - pum - pum)   When   we   come.
rum - pum - pum - pum)   On   my   drum?
rum - pum - pum - pum)   Me   and   my   drum.

A Pint of Judgment

ELIZABETH MORROW

You can give without loving, but you cannot love without giving.—AMY CARMICHAEL

The Tucker family made out lists of what they wanted for Christmas. They did not trust to the wisdom of aunts and uncles in such an important matter. By the first week in December everybody had written out what he or she hoped to receive.

Sally, who was seven, when she could only print had sent little slips of paper up the chimney with her desires plainly set forth. She had wondered sometimes if neatly written requests like Ellen's were not more effective than the printed ones. Ellen was eight. She had asked last year for a muff, and Santa had sent it.

Mother always explained that one should not expect to get all the things on the list; "Only what you want most, dear, and sometimes you have to wait till you are older for those."

For several years Sally had asked for a lamb, and she had almost given up hope of finding one tied to her stocking on Christmas morning. She had also asked for a white cat and a dove, and they had not come either. Instead, a bowl of goldfish had been received. Now she wrote so plainly that there was no excuse for misunderstandings like this.

Derek still printed his list, he was only six, and yet he had received an Indian suit the very first time he asked for it. It was puzzling.

The lists were useful too in helping one to decide what to make for Father and Mother and the others for Christmas. The little Tuckers had been brought up by their grandmother in the belief that a present you made yourself was far superior to one bought in a store. Mother always asked for a great many things the children could make. She was always wanting knitted washcloths, pincushion covers, blotters, and penwipers. Father needed pipe cleaners, calendars, and decorated matchboxes. This year Sally longed to do something quite different for her mother. She was very envious of Ellen, who had started a small towel as her present, and was pulling threads for a fringed end.

"Oh Ellen! How lovely that is!" she sighed. "It is a real grown-up present, just as if Aunt Elsie had made it."

"And it isn't half done yet," Ellen answered proudly. "Grandma is helping me with cross-stitch letters in blue and red for one end."

"If I could only make something nice like that! Can't you think of something for me?"

"A hemmed handkerchief?" suggested Ellen.

"Oh, no! Mother has lots of handkerchiefs."

"Yes, but when I gave her one for her birthday she said she had never had enough handkerchiefs. They were like asparagus."

"They don't look like asparagus," Sally replied, loath to criticize her mother but evidently confused. "Anyway, I don't want to give her a handkerchief."

"A penwiper?"

"No, I'm giving Father that."

"A new pincushion cover?"

"Oh no, Ellen. I'm sick of those presents. I want it to be a big—lovely—something, a great surprise."

Ellen thought a minute. She was usually resourceful, and she did not like to fail her little sister. They had both been earning money all through November and perhaps this was time to buy a present for Mother even if Grandma disapproved.

"I know that Mother has made out a new list," she said. "She and Father were laughing about it last night in the library. Let's go and see if it is there."

They found two papers on the desk, unmistakably lists. They were typewritten. Father's was very short: "Anything wrapped up in tissue paper with a red ribbon around it."

"Isn't Father funny?" giggled Ellen. "I'd like to fool him and do up a dead mouse for his stocking."

Mother had filled a full page with her wants. Ellen read out slowly:

Pair of Old English silver peppers
Fur coat
("Father will give her that.")
Umbrella
Robert Frost's *Poems*
Silk stockings
Muffin tins
Small watering pot for houseplants
Handkerchiefs
Guest towels
(" Aren't you glad she asked for
that?" Sally broke in.)
Knitted washcloths
A red pencil
A blue pencil
Ink eraser
Pen holders
Rubber bands
Hot water bag cover
A *quart of judgment*

This last item was scribbled in pencil at the bottom of the sheet.

As Ellen finished reading, she said with what Sally called her "little-mother air," "You needn't worry at all about Mother's present. There are lots of things here you could make for her. Couldn't you do a hot water bag cover if Grandma cut it out for you? I'm sure you could. You take a nice soft piece of old flannel—"

"No! No! Nothing made out of old flannel!" cried Sally. "That's such a baby thing. I want it to be different—and a great surprise. I wish I could give her the silver peppers. That's the first thing on her list; but I've only got two dollars and three cents in my bank, and I'm afraid that's not enough."

"Oh! It isn't the peppers she wants most!" cried Ellen. It's the last thing she wrote down, that 'quart of judgment.' I know for I heard her tell Father, 'I need that more than anything else, even a pint would help.' And then they both laughed."

"What is judgment?" asked Sally.

"It's what the judge gives: a judgment," her sister answered. "It must be something to do with the law."

"Then I know it would cost more than two dollars and three cents," said Sally. "Father said the other day that nothing was so expensive as the law."

"But she only asked for a pint," Ellen objected. "A pint of anything couldn't be very expensive, unless it was diamonds and rubies."

"She wanted a quart," Sally corrected. "And she just said that afterwards about a pint helping because she knew a whole quart would be too much for us to buy."

"A hot water bag cover would be lots easier," cautioned Ellen.

"I don't want it to be easy!" cried Sally. "I want it to be what she wants!"

"Well, perhaps you could get it cheap from Uncle John," Ellen suggested. "He's a lawyer—and he's coming to dinner tonight, so you could ask him."

Sally was not afraid to ask Uncle John anything. He never laughed at her or teased her as Uncle Tom sometimes did, and he always talked to her as if she were grown up. On any vexed question he always sided with her and Ellen. He had even been known to say before Mother that coconut cake was good for children and that seven-thirty for big girls of seven and eight was a disgracefully early bedtime. Sally drew him into the little library that evening and shut the door carefully.

"Is it something very important?" he asked as they seated themselves on the sofa.
"Yes," she answered. "Awfully important. It's a secret. You won't tell, will you?"

"It's, it's—Oh, Uncle John, what is judgment? I must get some."

"Judgment? That is an important question, my dear." Uncle John seemed puzzled for a moment. "And it is hard to answer. Why do you bother about that now? You have your whole life to get it. Come to me again when you're eighteen."

"But I can't wait so long. I must get it right away. Mother wants it for a Christmas present. She put on her list, 'A quart of judgment.' She said even a pint would help."

Uncle John laughed. He threw back his head and shouted. Sally had never seen him laugh so hard. He shook the sofa with his mirth and tears rolled down his cheeks. He didn't stop until he saw that Sally was hurt, and even then a whirlwind of

chuckles seized him occasionally.

"I'm not laughing at you, Sally darling," he explained at last, patting her shoulder affectionately, "but at your mother. She doesn't need judgment. She has it. She always has had it. She's a mighty fine woman—your mother. She must have put that on her list as a joke."

"Oh no! Excuse me, Uncle John," Sally protested. "She told Father she wanted it more than anything else. Wouldn't it be a good Christmas present?"

"Perfectly swell," her uncle answered. "The most useful. If you have any left over, give me some."

"Why, I was going to ask you to sell me some," Sally explained. "Ellen said you would surely have it."

Just then Mother called "Ellen! Sally! Bedtime. Hurry, dears. It's twenty minutes to eight already."

"Bother!" exclaimed Sally. "I'm always having to go to bed. But please tell me where I can get it. At Macy's? Delia is taking us to town tomorrow."

"No, my dear," he answered. "Macy sells almost everything but not that. It doesn't come by the yard."

"Girls!" Mother's voice again.

"Oh! Quick, Uncle John," whispered Sally. "Mother's coming. I'll have to go. Just tell me. What is judgment?"

"It is sense, Sally," he answered, quite solemn and serious now. "Common sense. But it takes a lot . . ." He could not finish the sentence, for at this point Mother opened the door and carried Sally off to bed.

The little girl snuggled down under the sheets very happily. Uncle John had cleared her mind of all doubt. She had only time for an ecstatic whisper to Ellen before Delia put out the light: "It's all right about Mother's present. Uncle John said it would be 'swell.'" Then she began to calculate: "If it is just cents, common cents, I have ever so many in my bank and I can earn some more. Perhaps I have enough already."

With this delicious hope she fell asleep.

The first thing after breakfast the next morning she opened her bank. It was in the shape of a fat man sitting in a chair. When you put a penny in his hand,

he nodded his head in gratitude as the money slipped into his safetybox. Sally unscrewed the bottom of this, and two dollars and three cents rolled out. It was not all in pennies. There were several nickels, three dimes, two quarters, and a fifty-cent piece. It made a rich-looking pile. Sally ran to the kitchen for a pint cup and then up to the nursery to pour her wealth into it. No one was there in the room to hear her cry of disappointment. The coins did not reach to the "Half" marked on the measure.

But there was still hope. The half dollar and quarters when they were changed would lift the level of course. She put all the silver into her pocket and consulted Ellen.

Her sister had passed the penny-bank stage and kept her money in a blue leather purse which was a proud possession. Aunt Elsie had given it to her last Christmas. It had two compartments and a small looking-glass, but there was very little money in it now. Ellen had already bought a good many presents. She was only able to change one quarter and one dime.

Grandma changed a dime and Sally had sixty pennies all together to put into the pint cup. They brought the pile up about an inch.

When father came home that night she asked him to change the fifty-cent piece, the quarter, and the three nickels, but he did not have ninety cents in pennies and he said that he could not get them until Monday, and now it was only Saturday.

"You understand, Sally," he explained looking down into his little daughter's anxious face, "you don't have any more money after this is changed. It only looks more."

"I know, but I want it that way," she answered.

On Monday night he brought her the change, and it made a full inch more of money in the cup. Still it was less than half a pint. Sally confided her discouragement to Ellen.

"Are you sure," asked her sister, "that it was this kind of present Mother wanted? She never asked for money before."

"I'm sure," Sally replied. "Uncle John said it was cents and that it would take a lot. Besides she prayed for it in church yesterday, so she must want it awfully."

"Prayed for it!" exclaimed Ellen in surprise.

"Yes. I heard her. It's that prayer we all say together. She asked God for 'two cents of all thy mercies.'"

"But if she wants a whole pint why did she only ask for 'two cents'?" demanded the practical Ellen.

"I don't know," Sally answered. "Perhaps she thought it would be greedy. Mother is never greedy."

For several days things were at a standstill. Ellen caught a cold and passed it on to Sally and Derek. They were all put to bed and could do very little Christmas work. There seemed no way of adding anything to the pint cup.

"Mother, how could I earn some money quickly before Christmas?" Sally asked the first day that she was up.

"You have already earned a good deal, dear," Mother said. "Do you really need more?"

"Yes, Mother, lots more."

"How about getting 100 in your number work? Father gives you a dime every time you do that."

"Yes," sighed Sally, "but it's very hard to get all the examples right. Don't you think when I get all right but one he might give me nine cents?"

"No," said Mother laughing. "Your father believes that nothing is good in arithmetic but 100."

She did earn one dime that way and then school closed, leaving no hope for anything more before Christmas.

On the twentieth of December there was a windfall. Aunt Elsie, who usually spent the holidays with them, was in the South and she sent Mother four dollars, one for each child for a Christmas present.

"She told me to buy something for you," Mother explained, "but I thought perhaps you might like to spend the money yourselves later on during vacation."

"Oh! I'd like my dollar right away!" cried Sally delightedly.

Aunt Elsie's gift brought the pennies in the pint cup a little above the half mark.

On the twenty-first Sally earned five cents by sweeping off the back porch. This had been a regular source of revenue in the fall, but when the dead leaves gave place to snow Mother forbade the sweeping. On the twenty-first there was no snow, and Sally was allowed to go out with her little broom.

On the twenty-second Ellen and Sally went to a birthday party, and Sally found a shiny bright dime in her piece of birthday cake. This helped a little. She and Ellen spent all their spare moments in shaking up the pennies in the pint measure—but they could not bring the level much above "One Half." Ellen was as excited over the plan now as Sally, and she generously added her last four cents to the pile.

On the twenty-third Sally made a final desperate effort. "Mother," she said, "Uncle John is coming to dinner again tonight. Do you think he would be willing to give me my birthday dollar now?"

Mother smiled as she answered slowly, "But your birthday isn't till June. Isn't it rather strange to ask for your present so long ahead? Where is all this money going to?"

"It's a secret! My special secret!" cried the little girl, taking her mother's reply for consent.

Uncle John gave her the dollar. She hugged and kissed him with delight, and he said, "Let me always be your banker, Sally."

When Father changed the birthday dollar into pennies he said, "You are getting to be a regular little miser, my dear. I don't understand it. Where is all this money going to?"

"That's just what Mother asked," Sally answered. "It's a secret. You'll know on Christmas.

Oh, Father, I think I have enough now!"

But she hadn't. The pennies seemed to melt away as they fell into the measure. She and Ellen took them all out three times and put them back again shaking them sideways and forwards, but it was no use. They looked a mountain on the nursery floor, but they shrank in size the moment they were put inside that big cup. The mark stood obstinately below "Three Quarters."

"Oh! Ellen!" sobbed Sally after the third attempt. "Not even a pint! It's a horrid mean little present! All my presents are horrid. I never can give nice things like you! Oh dear, what shall I do!"

"Don't cry, Sally, please don't," said Ellen, trying to comfort her little sister. "It's not a horrid present. It will look lovely when you put tissue paper around it and lots of red ribbon and a card. It sounds so much more than it looks; Ellen went on, giving the cup a vigorous jerk. "Why don't you print on your card 'Shake well before opening,' like our cough mixture?"

"I might," assented Sally, only partly reassured.

She had believed up to the last moment that she would be able to carry out her plan. It was vaguely associated in her mind with a miracle. Anything might happen at Christmastime, but this year she had hoped for too much. It was so late now however that there was nothing to do but make the outside of her gift look as attractive as possible. She and Ellen spent most of the afternoon before Christmas wrapping up their presents. The pint cup was a little awkward in shape; but they had it well covered, and the red satin ribbon gathered tight at the top before Grandma made the final bow. It was a real rosette, for Sally had asked for something special.

Christmas Eve was almost more fun than Christmas. The Tuckers made a ceremony of hanging up their stockings. The whole family formed a line in the upper hall with Father at the head, the youngest child on his back, and then they marched downstairs keeping step to a Christmas chant. It was a homemade nonsense verse with a chorus of "Doodley-doodley, doodley-doo!" which everybody shouted. By the time they reached the living room the line was in wild spirits.

The stockings were always hung in the same places. Father had the big armchair to the right of the fireplace and Mother the large mahogany chair opposite it, Lovey had a small white chair borrowed from the nursery. Derek tied his sock to the hook which usually held the fire tongs above the wood basket (it was a very inconvenient place, but he liked it) and Ellen and Sally divided the sofa.

After the stockings were put up, one of the children recited the Bible verses, "And there were in the same country shepherds abiding in the field, keeping watch over their flock by night," through "Mary kept all these things and pondered them in her heart." Sally had said the verses last Christmas, Ellen the year before, and now it was Derek's turn. He only forgot once and Ellen prompted him softly.

Then they all sang "Holy Night" and Father read "'Twas the Night Before Christmas." Last of all, the children distributed their gifts for the family with a great many stern directions: "Mother, you won't look at this till tomorrow, will you? Father, you promise not to peek?" Then they went up to bed, and by morning Father and Mother and Santa Claus had the stockings stuffed full of things.

It went off as usual this year but through all the singing and the shouting Sally had twinges of disappointment thinking of Mother's unfinished present. She had squeezed it into Mother's stocking with some difficulty. Then came Ellen's lovely towel and on top of that Derek's calendar which he had made in school.

There was a family rule at the Tuckers' that

stockings were not opened until after breakfast. Mother said that presents on an empty stomach were bad for temper and digestion, and though it was hard to swallow your cereal Christmas morning, the children knew it was no use protesting.

The first sight of the living room was wonderful. The place had completely changed over night. Of course the stockings were knobby with unknown delights, and there were packages everywhere, on the tables and chairs, and on the floor big express boxes that had come from distant places, marked "Do Not Open Until Christmas."

Some presents are of such unmistakable shape that they cannot be hidden. Last year Derek had jumped right onto his rocking horse shouting, It's mine! I know it's mine!" This morning he caught sight of a drum and looked no further. Lovey fell upon a white plush bunny. A lovely pink parasol was sticking out of the top of Sally's stocking and Ellen had a blue one. They just unfurled them over their heads and then watched Father and Mother unwrapping their presents.

The girls felt Derek and Lovey were very young because they emptied their stockings without a look toward the two big armchairs. That was the most thrilling moment, when your own offering came to view and Mother said, "Just what I wanted!" or Father, "How did you know I needed a penwiper?"

Mother always opened the children's presents first. She was untying the red ribbon on Ellen's towel now and reading the card which said "Every stitch a stitch of love." As she pulled off the tissue paper she exclaimed, "What beautiful work! What exquisite little stitches! Ellen, I am proud of you. This is a charming guest towel. Thank you dear so much."

"Grandma marked the cross-stitch for me," explained Ellen, "but I did all the rest myself."

Sally shivered with excitement as Mother's hand went down into her stocking again and tugged at the tin cup.

Here is something very heavy," she said. "I can't guess what it is, and the card says 'Merry Christmas to Mother from Sally. Shake well before opening.' Is it medicine or cologne?"

Nobody remembered just what happened after that. Perhaps Grandma's bow was not tied tightly enough, perhaps Mother tilted the cup as she shook it, but in a moment all the pennies were on the floor. They rolled everywhere, past the chairs, into the grate, under the sofa, and on to the remotest corners of the room. There was a terrific scramble. Father and Mother and Ellen and Sally and Derek, even Grandma and Lovey got down on their hands and knees to pick them up. They bumped elbows and knocked heads together and this onrush sent the coins flying everywhere. The harder they were chased the more perversely they hid themselves. Out of the hubbub Mother cried, "Sally dear, what is this? I don't understand. All your Christmas money for me? Darling, I can't take it."

Sally flung herself into her mother's arms with a sob. "Oh! you must!" she begged. "I'm sorry it's not a whole pint. I tried so hard. You said, you said, you wanted it most of all."

"Most of all?"

"Yes, judgment, cents. Uncle John said it was cents. You said even a pint would help. Won't half a pint be some good?"

Father and Mother and Grandma all laughed then. Father laughed almost as hard as Uncle John did when he first heard of Mother's list, and he declared that he was going to take Sally into the bank as a partner. But Mother lifted the little girl into her lap and whispered, "It's the most wonderful present I ever had. There's nothing so wonderful as sense—except love."

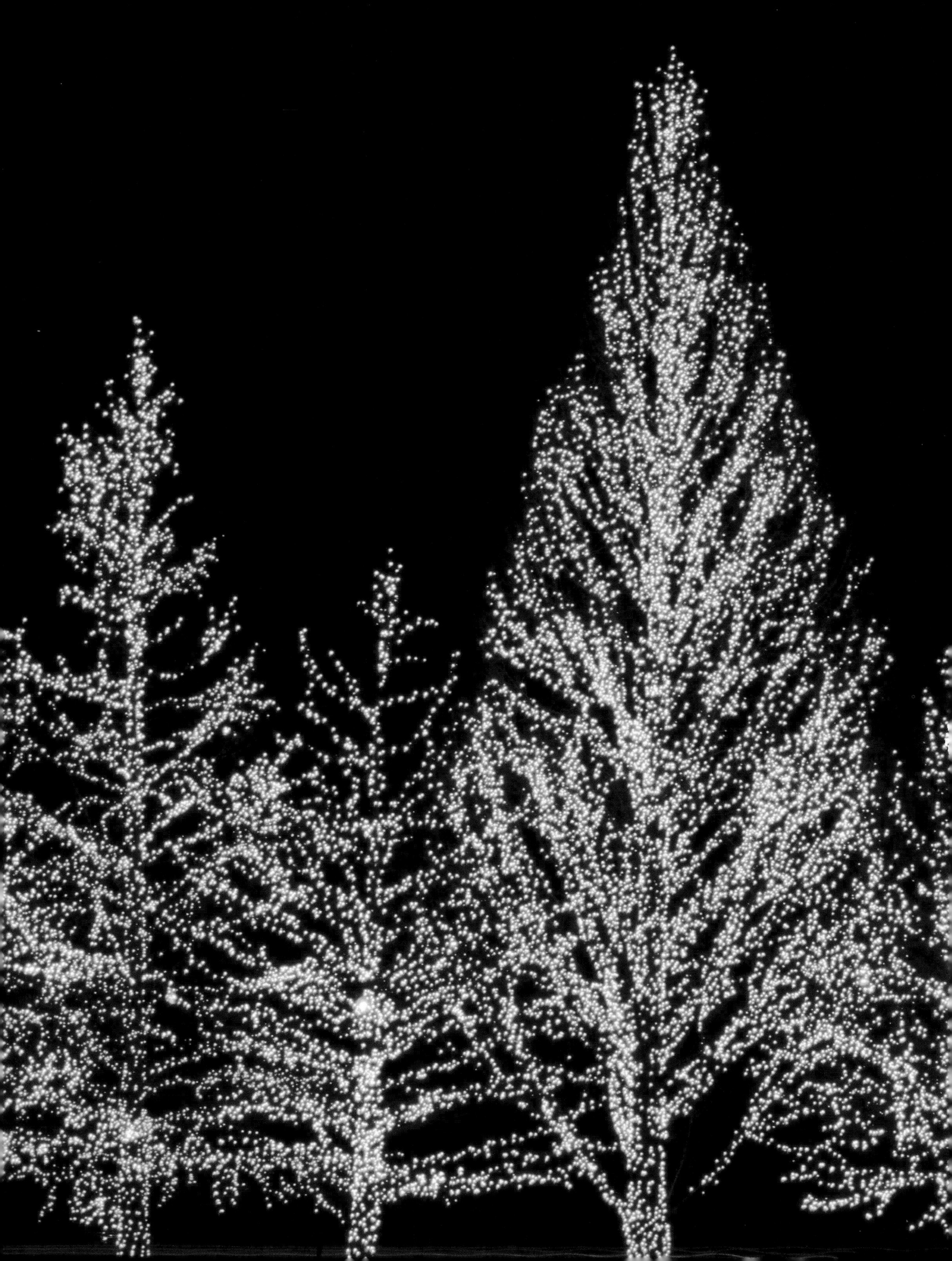

Christmas Chime

Old lady in black bonnet,
    Bell she'd ting-a-ling—
I flung in half a dollar
    To hear her pot go *ping!*

Remembered then. Felt funny.
    Heart just started stopping.
I'd thrown away the money
    I had saved for shopping!

And yet my mother wasn't
    Mad. Called that *ping* of the pot
As merry a Christmas present
    As any she'd ever got.
          X. J. KENNEDY

While Stars of Christmas Shine

While stars of Christmas shine,
    Lighting the skies,
Let only loving looks,
    Beam from our eyes.

While bells of Christmas ring,
    Joyous and clear,
Speak only happy words,
    All love and cheer.

Give only loving gifts,
    And in love take;
Gladden the poor and sad
    For love's dear sake.
          EMILIE POULSSON

Give It to Somebody Who Needs It

MARJORIE HOLMES

here's nobody quite like a son. . . .

A certain mother in Virginia made the usual request of her children: "Now please make out your Christmas lists so your father and I can start shopping. We have to know what you want."

In a day or so the lists were presented, filled with the inevitable requests for expensive things. One message surprised them, however. It was in the form of a note from their seventeen-year-old son: "This year please take the money you would ordinarily spend on me and give it to some poor family or institution that helps kids," he asked.

"Oh, boy, here we go; he's coming down with hippieitis," they thought. And told each other, "That's out of the question; it would be too awful, everybody else opening presents Christmas morning and him without anything to unwrap."

But when they confronted their son, he explained: "Well, every time I ask for something you say, 'But that costs sixty dollars,' or 'That costs one hundred dollars.' Sure, I generally get it, but first I've got to be told how much it costs and maybe that's a good thing because I don't really need anything and I can't think of anything I really want. So why not take all the money you'd spend on me just because it's Christmas, and give it to somebody who does need and want things?"

As they gazed at him they realized he was serious. He preferred the warm and wonderful knowledge that somewhere, other needier kids were getting the gifts that would only be superfluous to him.

By not giving their son packages to open on Christmas morning, they would be giving him something far more valuable than they could every buy in a store.

Angel on a Doorstep

SHIRLEY BACHELDER

May the joy and spirit of Christmas stay with us now and forever.—PETER MARSHALL

When Ben delivered milk to my cousin's home that morning, he wasn't his usual sunny self. The slight, middle-aged man seemed in no mood for talking.

It was late November 1962, and as a newcomer to Lawndale, California, I was delighted that milkmen still brought bottles of milk to doorsteps. In the weeks that my husband, kids, and I had been staying with my cousin while house-hunting, I had come to enjoy Ben's jovial repartee.

Today, however, he was the epitome of gloom as he dropped off his wares from his wire carrier. It took slow, careful questioning to extract the story from him. With some embarrassment, he told me two customers had left town without paying their bills, and he would have to cover the losses. One of the debtors owed only ten dollars, but the other was seventy-nine dollars in arrears and had left no forwarding address. Ben was distraught at his stupidity for allowing this bill to grow so large.

"She was a pretty woman," he said, "with six children and another on the way. She was always saying, 'I'm going to pay you soon, when my husband gets a second job.' I believed her. What a fool I was! I thought I was doing a good thing, but I've learned my lesson. I've been had!"

All I could say was, "I'm so sorry."

The next time I saw him, his anger seemed worse. He bristled as he talked about the messy young ones who had drunk up all his milk. The charming family had turned into a parcel of brats.

I repeated my condolences and let the matter rest. But when Ben left, I found myself caught up in his problem and longed to help. Worried that this incident would sour a warm person, I mulled over what to do. Then, remembering that Christmas was coming, I thought of what my grandmother used to say: "When someone has taken from you, give it to them, and then you can never be robbed."

The next time Ben delivered milk, I told him I had a way to

make him feel better about the seventy-nine dollars.

"Nothing will do that," he said, "but tell me anyway."

"Give the woman the milk. Make it a Christmas present to the kids who needed it."

"Are you kidding?" he replied. "I don't even get my wife a Christmas gift that expensive."

"You know the Bible says, 'I was a stranger and you took me in.' You just took her in with all her little children."

"Don't you mean she took me in? The trouble with you is, it wasn't your seventy-nine dollars."

I let the subject drop, but I still believed in my suggestion.

We'd joke about it when he'd come. "Have you given her the milk yet?" I'd say.

"No," he'd snap back, "but I'm thinking of giving my wife a seventy-nine dollar present, unless another pretty mother starts playing on my sympathies."

Every time I'd ask the question, it seemed he lightened up a bit more.

Then, six days before Christmas, it happened. He arrived with a tremendous smile and a glint in his eyes. "I did it!" he said. "I gave her the milk as a Christmas present. It wasn't easy, but what did I have to lose? It was gone, wasn't it?"

"Yes," I said, rejoicing with him. "But you've got to really mean it in your heart."

"I know. I do. And I really feel better. That's why I have this good feeling about Christmas. Those kids had lots of milk on their cereal just because of me."

The holidays came and went. On a sunny January morning two weeks later, Ben almost ran up the walk. "Wait till you hear this," he said, grinning.

He explained he had been on a different route, covering for another milkman. He heard his name being called, looked over his shoulder and saw a woman running down the street, waving money. He recognized her immediately—the woman with all the kids, the one who didn't pay her bill. She was carrying an infant in a tiny blanket, and the woman's long brown hair kept getting in her eyes.

"Ben, wait a minute!" she shouted. "I've got money for you."

Ben stopped the truck and got out.

"I'm so sorry," she said. "I really have been meaning to pay you." She explained that her husband had come home one night and announced he'd found a cheaper apartment. He'd also gotten a night job. With all that had happened, she'd forgotten to leave a forwarding address. "But I've been saving," she said. "Here's twenty dollars toward the bill."

"That's all right," Ben replied. "It's been paid."

"Paid?" she exclaimed. "What do you mean? Who paid it?"

"I did."

She looked at him as if he were the Angel Gabriel and started to cry.

"Well," I asked, "what did you do?"

"I didn't know what to do, so I put an arm around her. Before I knew what was happening, I started to cry, and I didn't have the foggiest idea what I was crying about. Then I thought of all those kids having milk on their cereal, and you know what? I was really glad you talked me into this."

"You didn't take the twenty dollars?"

"Heck no," he replied indignantly. "I gave her the milk as a Christmas present, didn't I?"

Giving

May all your gifts at Christmas be
Bright packages beneath your tree,
Filled with blessings from above
And cheerful smiles from those you love;
Filled with happiness untold,
Lasting friendships, new and old;
Peace and joy, contentment, too,
Enough to last the whole year through.

JAMES E. FEIG

The Holly's Up

The holly's up, the house is all bright,
The tree is ready, the candles alight:
Rejoice and be glad, all children tonight!

Let every house be ready tonight—
The children gathered, the candles alight—
That music to hear, to see that sight.

P. CORNELIUS

Christmas Sweets

Gingersnaps

2¼ cup all-purpose flour, divided
1 cup light brown sugar, packed
¼ teaspoon salt
¾ cup shortening
¼ cup molasses
1 egg

1 teaspoon baking soda
1 teaspoon ground ginger
1 teaspoon ground cinnamon
½ teaspoon ground cloves
¼ cup granulated sugar

Preheat oven to 375°. In a large bowl, combine 1¼ cups of the flour, brown sugar, salt, shortening, molasses, egg, baking soda, ginger, cinnamon, and cloves. Beat until thoroughly mixed. Stir in an additional 1 cup flour. Shape dough into 1-inch balls. Roll balls in sugar and place 2 inches apart on an ungreased cookie sheet. Bake 8 to 10 minutes or until the edges are set and tops are crackled. Cool on cookie sheet for 1 minute. Remove to wire rack to cool. Store in a tightly covered container. Makes 4 dozen cookies.

Holiday Kringle

1	package dry yeast	½	teaspoon salt
¼	cup warm water	½	cup butter, cut into pieces
2	cups all-purpose flour	½	cup milk
1½	tablespoons sugar	1	egg yolk

In a small bowl, dissolve yeast in warm water (110°-115°); set aside in a warm place. In a large bowl, combine flour, sugar, and salt, mixing well. With a pastry blender, cut in butter until the mixture is the consistency of cornmeal. Set aside. In a saucepan, heat milk to lukewarm; blend in egg yolk. Add yeast. Gradually add milk-yeast mixture to the flour mixture, blending lightly with a fork until all particles are moistened. Cover with plastic wrap and foil; refrigerate 2 to 24 hours. Prepare fillings.

Preheat oven to 400° F. Lightly grease two cookie sheets. Punch dough down. Divide into 2 parts. On a lightly floured surface, roll each half to an 18- x 6-inch rectangle. Spread filling down the middle of the dough, spreading it to a 3-inch width. (If using the butter pecan filling, then sprinkle pecans on top). Fold one long side of dough over the filling. Fold other side, overlapping dough about 1½ inches. Pinch edge and ends to seal. Place seam-side down on cookie sheet. Form into a circle, pinching ends together. Cover; let rise in a warm place until light and puffy, 15 to 20 minutes. Bake 15 to 20 minutes until golden brown. Remove from cookie sheets and cool. Sift powdered sugar over the top before serving.

Poppy Seed Filling

¼	cup popppy seed
2	tablespoons milk
2	tablespoons melted butter
1	teaspoon cinnamon
1	teaspoon lemon zest

Grind or mash poppy seed. Combine all ingredients and mix well. Set aside. Makes filling for 1 Kringle.

Butter Pecan Filling

¼	cup packed brown sugar
½	cup butter
¼	teaspoon cinnamon
1	cup chopped pecans

Combine all ingredients and mix well. Set aside. Makes filling for 1 Kringle.

Our Gifts to Our Children

What do we give to our children? First we give them the most precious of all gifts: the principles of brotherly love and the love of God, as taught so many years ago by Christ, whose birth we celebrate.

We give them our attention; for one day it will be too late.

We give them a sense of value. A place for the individual in the scheme of things, with all that accrues to the individual: self-reliance, courage, conviction, self-respect and the respect of others.

We give them a sense of humor because laughter leavens life.

We give them the meaning of discipline. If we falter at discipline, life will do it for us.

We give them the will to work. Satisfying work is not the lasting joy, but knowing that a job is well-done.

We give them the talent for sharing. That it's not so much that we give, as to what we share.

We give them the love of justice—the bulwark against violence and oppression, and the repository of human dignity.

We give them the passion for truth: founded on precept of example, truth is the beginning of every good thing; the power and the faith engendering mutual trust.

We give them the beacon of hope which lights all darkness.

We give them the knowledge of being loved. Beyond the demand for reciprocity, praise or blame, for those loved are never lost.

What shall we give the children? The open sky, the brown earth, the leafy trees, the golden sand, the blue water, the stars in their courses, and the awareness of these: birdsongs, butterflies, clouds and rainbows, sunlight, moonlight, firelight; a large hand reaching down for a small hand, impromptu praise, an unexpected kiss, a straight answer, the glisten of enthusiasm and the sense of wonder, long days to be merry in and nights without fear, and the memory of a good home.

These things we shall give the children.

AUTHOR UNKNOWN

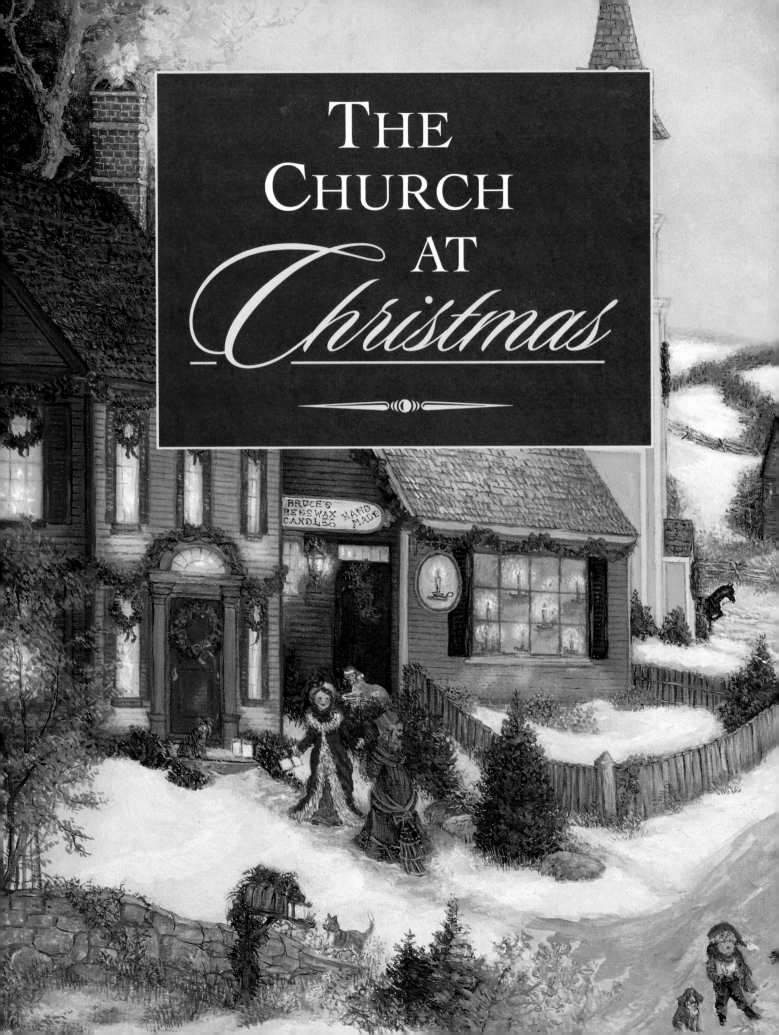

THE
CHURCH
AT
Christmas

Oh, How Joyfully

J. FALK

SICILIAN HYMN

1. Oh, how joy - ful - ly, Oh, how mer - ri - ly
3. Oh, how joy - ful - ly, Oh, how mer - ri - ly

Christ - mas comes with its grace di - vine!
Christ - mas comes with its peace di - vine!

Grace a - gain is beam - ing, Christ the world re - deem - ing:
Peace on earth is reign - ing, Christ our peace re - gain - ing;

Hail, ye Christ - ians, hail the joy - ous Christ - mas - time!
Hail, ye Christ - ians, hail the joy - ous Christ - mas - time!

The Little White Church

Starlight illumines the little white church,
In a peace-loving valley beside a bright stream.
The steeple cross sparkles with radiant gold,
In the light of the stars and a yellow moonbeam . . .
The magic of singing is heard in the air,
Not the grand alleluiahs of great city choirs,
But the loveliest kind that ascends from the soul,
Resounding with sweetness that thrills and inspires.
Peace and contentment steal through the soft light,
Into the church and to all who believe
In the virtue of goodness, the power of faith,
In the beauty and sacredness of Christmas Eve.
Help us, dear Father, to build in our hearts
A little white church bathed in tranquil moonlight,
Where we may find solace, contentment, and joy,
Not only at Christmas but all through the night.

ROSE MARIE OVERMAN

An Old Country Church

There's an old country church 'way back in memory
That I never expect to visit again,
But I'll never forget it—the church in the valley
Where the old and the young for Christmas would rally.

There was always a tree and candles aglow
To cast a shadow on the glistening snow,
As a good old Santa dressed in his best
Would find a present for every guest.

I still seem to hear the bell that would ring,
And a message of good tidings its tolling would bring,
As in sleighs filled with straw and from miles around
Came gay country folks in answer to its sound.

'Twas there at the church that true friendships were born,
Surviving many holidays that have passed and gone,
As good folks joined together to frolic and play
And be happy and cheerful on a Christmas Day.

P. F. FREEMAN

Home Church Christmas

DAVE ENGEL

When I think of a church at Christmas, it often is of an old wooden church in a smaller town than this: the fundamentalist Evangelical United Brethren, home-church of my father and mother. My impression of the building itself is of a simple, steepled structure.

I remember stained-glass windows donated "in loving memory of" and hard wooden pews in which the same people sat the same place every time I saw them, which was every time I went. Missing church on Sunday was unthinkable if not actually sinful.

It was not as clear to me then as it now is that the speech and demeanor of the parishioners is determined by their being German. The white foreheads and rough hands tell me clearly, though, that they are farmers who work almost all the time, who abide close to earth and animals. The men and boys often smell of manure and silage, having been to the barn Sunday morning, as every morning, for chores. They wear the same simple gray suits they always have worn.

A few are strangers to me. Many belong to my own family of uncles and aunts, cousins and grandparents. Others are elderly men and women I often meet at the church, whose relationship to me is obscure. They seem to be from another time. Some are children I don't really know.

Many of the Brethren are as strict as my own relatives. There is to be no drinking, no smoking, and no card-playing. Social life seems to be a matter of restrained if good-humored sobriety. It's early to bed, early to rise.

Normally, we visit the old church by day but, at Christmas, we go at night.

On the snowy drive in from the farm, Mom leads carols, such as "Silent Night" and "O Holy Night." Alighting from Grandpa's Hudson at the church, Mom and Dad happily greet friends and family from way back when they too, lived here.

Young and old show genuine enthusiasm. For the children, there are treats to come. For the parents, the burden of husbandry has lifted. A more peaceful occupation shows in their faces.

The sanctuary has changed too. With other lights dimmed, modest Christmas ornamentation and a tree have appeared. Figures on the windows reflect red and green light from within. An organist plays soft Christmas melodies rather than the more strident hymns of Sunday.

From somewhere on the left, I watch as darkness comes over the room and

angels appear, their wings of gift cardboard and their coat-hanger halos just as amazing as feathers or fins.

Other children of farmers have changed into bathrobes. They carry staffs and wands, and have adopted a new tongue, speaking in terms like "behold" and "glad tidings" and "a king is born."

In the old church, among people who normally don't encourage a lot of fooling around, these children have got up to put on a show. To the little boy in the dark, it is more than prestidigitation.

Christmas Is Coming

D. H. Lawrence

Gradually there gathered the feeling of expectation. Christmas was coming. In the shed, at nights, a secret candle was burning, a sound of veiled voices was heard. The boys were learning the old mystery play of St. George and Beelzebub. Twice a week, by lamplight, there was choir practice in the church, for the learning of old carols Brangwen wanted to hear. The girls went to these practices. Everywhere was a sense of mystery and rousedness. Everybody was preparing for something.

The time came near, the girls were decorating the church, with cold fingers binding holly and fir and yew about the pillars, till a new spirit was in the church, the stone broke out into dark, rich leaf, the arches put forth their æuds, and cold flowers rose to blossom in the dim, mystic atmosphere. Ursula must weave mistletoe over the door, and over the screen, and hang a silver dove from a sprig of yew, till dusk came down, and the church was like a grove. . . .

The expectation grew more tense. The star was risen into the sky. The songs, the carols were ready to hail it. The star was this sign in the sky. Earth too should give a sign. As evening drew on, hearts beat fast with anticipation, hands were full of ready gifts. There were the tremulously expectant words of the church service, the night was past and the morning was come, the gifts were given and received, joy and peace made a flapping of wings in each heart, there was a great burst of carols, the Peace of the world had dawned, strife had passed away, every hand was linked in hand, every heart was singing.

Christmas in the Parsonage

HARTZELL SPENCE

Once in the year, and only once, the whole world stands still to celebrate the Advent of a life.—AUTHOR UNKNOWN

Christmas always was an exciting holiday. The family was a unit as at no other time; and Father, who throughout the year had been big brother and uncle to the entire community, was remembered by scores of parishioners as though he belonged to their own households.

One of our greatest Christmases occurred at Fort Dodge. It was the last of the old-fashioned Yuletide festivals, for war had come before the winter of 1914, and after the war Christmas was not the same.

In 1913 the merchant had not yet become the beneficiary; Christ in the manger was still worshipped. Most of the people of Fort Dodge made their own gifts, supplementing them by such items as sleds and skates, which they could not handily produce at home. The parsonage celebration began two weeks earlier than that of our neighbors because of the ceremony of packing a box for our Canadian relatives. A week's lull followed, until a box arrived from Canada, after which we turned to preparations for the church Christmas; we were not permitted to forget that first place was reserved for the Christ Child, whose birthday the holy day was. We children learned verses and attended rehearsals for the Christmas pageant. A few days before Christmas, a committee appeared at the parsonage with tubs of candy and nuts and packed sacks for Santa Claus to give every member of the Sunday School on Christmas Eve. We loved this, because any candy left over was ours.

Then downtown on the day before Christmas went the whole family to select the Christmas tree. Father examined it for durability, mother for size, we children for symmetry. We went to Woolworth's to augment the ornaments saved from year to year. Eileen, Fraser, and I would have run riot here had not father and mother patiently curbed our extravagance both in money and taste. If Mother shook her head, we rejected a gaudy ornament in favor of one more conventional; if father frowned, we were overreaching the budget.

Home again with our booty, we shared the intoxicating excitement of dressing the tree, which father enjoyed to the extent of writing his sermon on a clipboard in the living room instead of in his study. When the ornaments were in place, we opened the big bundle from the Canadian relatives and hefted, rattled, and sniffed the individual packets for possible identification, Father as curious as the rest of us. At the same time, we helped Father and Mother to sort packages from other towns where Father had served as pastor, and we arranged the offerings from his parishioners in Fort Dodge.

In the evening we went to the church and after the Christmas Eve service hurried home to appear in the window when the choir came by to sing carols.

Christmas morning we were up early. Church members began to call at seven o'clock and continued to drop in throughout the day, bringing gifts and messages. There were a few presents we could count on: the Mohnike girls' homemade candy, Tony Roffel's cut glass or Haviland, Mr. McCutcheon's barrel of apples. Father waited anxiously for the appearance of the Men's Brotherhood, hoping that their remembrance would be in cash, but it wasn't; they contributed a leather chair.

By noon the tables overflowed with presents: handmade lace, wearing apparel, preserved fruits, cakes, candies, oranges, nine scarves, four pairs of mittens, and for Father— seven pairs of knitted socks with ties to match. The gifts were tokens of love from men and women who had no other way of expressing their gratitude and devotion to the pastor who counseled them, freed their children from escapades, solved their domestic problems, found employment for them, and lent them money.

People who were that generous with their preacher did not forget his children. We received candy enough to last, with careful hoarding, for six weeks or more and many games, which Father inspected carefully to be sure that they could not be utilized for gambling. When he carried one to the furnace, we didn't mind; what was one among a dozen.

Christmas Bells

The Bells

Hear the sledges with the bells—
Silver bells!
What a world of merriment their melody foretells!
How they tinkle, tinkle, tinkle,
In the icy air of night!
While the stars that oversprinkle
All the heavens, seem to twinkle
With a crystalline delight;
Keeping time, time, time,
In a sort of Runic rhyme,
To the tintinabulation that so musically wells
From the bells, bells, bells, bells,
Bells, bells, bells—
From the jingling and the tinkling of the bells.

EDGAR ALLEN POE

Song

Why do the bells of Christmas ring?
Why do little children sing?
Once a lovely star,
Seen by shepherds from afar,
Gently moved until its light
Made a manger's cradle bright.

There a darling baby lay,
Pillowed soft upon the hay,
And its mother sang and smiled:
"This is Christ, the Holy Child!"
Therefore the bells for Christmas ring,
Therefore little children sing.

EUGENE FIELD

I Heard the Bells

I heard the bells on Christmas Day
Their old familiar carols play,
    And wild and sweet
    The words repeat
Of peace on earth, goodwill to men.

And thought how, as the day had come,
The belfries of all Christendom
    Had rolled along
    The unbroken song
Of peace on earth, goodwill to men.

And in despair I bowed my head;
"There is no peace on earth," I said,
    "For hate is strong
    And mocks the song
Of peace on earth, goodwill to men."

Then pealed the bells more loud and deep:
"God is not dead, nor doth He sleep;
    The wrong shall fail,
    The right prevail
With peace on earth, goodwill to men."

HENRY WADSWORTH LONGFELLOW

Bells

The church bells at Christmas-time
Ring all about the town;
The gay folk at Christmas-time
Go walking up and down;
They smile at me, they smile at you,
The streets and squares are smiling too.

In every house at Christmas-time
Are pretty sights to see;
And strange things at Christmas-time
Do grow upon a tree;
And one for me and one for you,
And isn't it a sweet to-do?

ROSE FYLEMAN

When the Bells Ring Out

'Tis Christmastime when the bells ring out,
And the thrill of their fairy chime
Sings to a world of a Babe, newborn,
In that glad old Christmastime;

Sings to the heart "Look up, look up,
To the skies that bend above,
Look up from the shadows that dim the road
To the star-strewn way of love!"

When the bells peal out on a world of white,
O'er mountaintop and plain,
Then it's holly time, it's happy time,
For it's Christmastime again!

WALTER S. WHEELER

A Christmas Tapestry

PAUL E. ERTEL

I have always thought of Christmas as a good time; a kind, forgiving, generous, pleasant time; a time when men and women seem to open their hearts freely; and so I say, "God bless Christmas."—CHARLES DICKENS

An old, dried-up sacristy in an old, dried-up church. Pastor Fulton sat at the old, dried-up desk and penciled in a few last-minute changes in his sermon. In exactly one hour the Christmas Eve Service of Holy Communion would begin, the final service of his ministry, for soon after Christmas he would leave Brudersburg to retire in a warmer climate.

There, at that beloved desk, which had been handwrought in the old country, and brought to Trinity Church in time for its day of dedication nearly two hundred years ago, he, as his predecessors, had faithfully inscribed all the parish records: births, baptisms, confirmations, weddings, membership transfers, deaths, offerings, expenditures, and all sorts of historical data.

He bowed his head and closed his eyes, and the present bowed in awe to the past, but that huge bulldozer waiting so maliciously out there beside the church forbade any thought of a future.

At the time of its founding in 1787, Trinity Church had lifted up high above Brudersburg a great inspiring cross, and this had become the landmark of the city. In recent years, however, this had been all but lost among the towering new office buildings crowding in about it.

For a century and a half this great church had provided a many-faceted ministry to the area, but with the vast expansion of the city, and the flight of so many to the suburbs, the membership had declined from a peak of more than a thousand to less than a hundred. Its once-strong Sunday School could not survive the loss of its children and young people. Its choirs, for many years the pride of Brudersburg, had long been silent. Only the willingness of its talented and dedicated organist, Helen Kirche, to play for the Sunday Services without pay kept the sound of music in the sanctuary. The once-mighty organ was frequently out of order, and on such occasions the faltering voices of its few remaining members did not contribute much to the mood of worship.

Asher, the aging sexton, who knew and loved every nook and cranny of the church, and who had always insisted that he be called the sexton rather than the janitor, the caretaker, or the custodian, had for nearly a decade provided his services purely as a labor of love.

The building was in need of extensive repair, but the small membership could in no way afford it. In fact, the church would have been without a pastor for several years had not Pastor Fulton been willing to accept whatever was to be had, including a small subsidy from The Inner City Fund of the denomination, never quite ceasing to hope that, somehow the church might experience renewal.

During the early years of his ministry he had always had the manger scene with the Holy Family at the Christmas Eve Service. How often in recent weeks his memory had returned to that Christmas Eve Service thirty years before when Mary and Joseph and the Baby Jesus had made this service come alive for the last time; but even then attendance was declining.

His custom had been to invite the parents of the newest baby of the church to bring their child and serve as the Holy Family. However, during that whole year only one child had been born to a member family. Indeed, how well he remembered his coming! At one o'clock in the morning of August 1, 1948, he had been called to the hospital to baptize the newborn son of Joe and Marian Neubel, for the doctors believed that the child could not live through the night; and were he to survive at all, he was almost certain to be handicapped both physically and men-

tally throughout his life. The precious little boy, struggling to live, could not be removed from the special care unit in which he had been placed, so Pastor Fulton could only extend his hand momentarily into the unit, touch the little one's forehead with a tiny bit of water, and say, "Christopher Eugene Neubel, I baptize you in the name of the Father, and of the Son, and of the Holy Spirit, Amen."

Two weeks later the new mother was dismissed from the hospital, but baby Christopher, whose life was suspended as by a thread, remained there. Several weeks later he was dismissed, but the quality of his future was very uncertain. Pastor Fulton visited the Neubels every few days, and shared their joy and their concern.

Early in December Joe was notified by the company for which he worked that on February 1 of the new year he would be transferred to its office on the West Coast. This came as both a shock and a joy to the Neubels; a shock because of Christopher's health, but a joy because with the larger income, they could better care for him. All of this Joe and Marian shared with their pastor, and he was present when they made their final decision to move.

"Who knows?" he said, "This may be God's way of helping both you and Christopher through these times."

Several days before Christmas, Pastor Fulton phoned the Neubels and asked if they could see him a few minutes that evening. "We certainly can," they told him. "We'll be looking for you."

A few hours later, as they sat in the Neubels' living room, Pastor Fulton said, "My visit this evening is for a very special purpose. For all the years I have been at Trinity Church I have had the parents of the newest baby in the church bring their little one and serve as the

Holy Family at our Christmas Eve Service. Christopher is not only the newest baby this year, but the only one. I am inviting you to bring him to the service this Christmas Eve and serve as the Holy Family. I am aware of all the reasons you might have not to do this, but I have what I believe is a very good reason to do it."

"And what reason is that?" asked Joe.

"Yes," said Marian, "It must be a very good reason."

"I believe it is," said the pastor. "There are many ways to pray. Most of our prayers are spoken with words. Sometimes we only think our prayers. There are many symbolic ways to pray, such as kneeling, bowing the head, folding the hands, and closing the eyes. During most of my life, I have prayed by embodying my prayers in meaningful acts. Across the years I have chosen some rather difficult acts, and have lifted them up before God very much as I lift up the bread and wine at the Holy Sacrament. Many times I have felt His presence very near, and His guidance very strong.

"My invitation is to bring Christopher to this Christmas Eve Service and serve as the Holy Family, not as a favor to me, although it would be that, nor as an act of love to the church, although of course, it would be that. I suggest that you do this as an acted prayer of thanks that your little boy has survived these first difficult months; and that in this way you may share with our Father your hope that with the passing of the years, he may know all the blessings of health, happiness, and love."

The Neubels drew deep breaths and wondered what they should do.

"I shall go now," said their pastor, "and give you an opportunity to think about it. When you have made your decision, let me know."

The Neubels thought long and seriously about this. They even sought the counsel of their doctor, that they might make the proper decision. A few days later they phoned Pastor Fulton and agreed to do as he had suggested, "providing Christopher is as well on Christmas Eve as now." Their pastor thanked them warmly, for this would be a time of joy to everyone.

But all of this was now thirty years ago. His immediate concern was this, the final service of his ministry.

At the service the previous Christmas Eve the gracious old sanctuary had been host to only thirty-four people, but he had reminded them that, compared with the number at the manger in Bethlehem, they were a rather large gathering.

Since then, the Resident Bishop and his advisors had made a thorough study of Trinity Church and its problems, and had reluctantly decided that at the beginning of the next year, the building should be removed, and the ground turned over to the city to build a parking garage.

As he brooded over all this, and his retirement from the ministry, Pastor Fulton was disturbed by an urgent knocking at the sacristy door. It was Helen, the organist. She had come to the church a bit early to rehearse her music, but the organ had gone dead.

Pastor Fulton hurried to the blower room in the basement, threw off his coat and began going over the mechanism in search of the cause. The fuse and the switch were both intact, but the blower refused to work. Using such tools as were available, he searched feverishly, until half an hour later he discovered a broken wire, and working very carefully, repaired it with only a few minutes to go before the service was to begin. He ran to the kitchen to wash up, hoping to come to the Holy Sacrament with clean hands as well as a pure heart, and was rewarded with the sound of organ music coming from the sanctuary.

While Pastor Fulton was at work in the blower room, Asher, the sexton, had noticed a

special couple making its difficult way up the church steps from the cold winter night. The young mother was carrying a small baby wrapped in warm blankets. Her husband was assisted in his climb by a pair of sophisticated crutches, but as he came through the door his face was covered with perspiration, for he had made it up the steps only with great effort.

The old sexton held the door for them and welcomed them to the service. Sensing suddenly that this young family was not only burdened with a serious problem, but blessed with an incredible possibility, Asher urged them to follow

him, and led them directly to the sacristy. He told them how for thirty years there had not been a Holy Family at the Christmas Eve Service. If they would consent to serve as such tonight he could supply the proper garments, for they were still intact in their leather bag in the sacristy closet. To his pleasure, they readily consented.

When Pastor Fulton finally returned to the sacristy, he noticed some coats lying on the desk, but he had not time to ask questions. Off came his coat; on went his vestments; but in his hurry he left his sermon notes lying on the desk. Whispering a prayer for guidance and strength as he

moved into the sanctuary, he was completely astounded, for there sat a congregation that filled the church to the very front pew. What he didn't know was that the good Bishop had engineered a movement among all the churches of the city to send a few of their own members to this final service in Trinity Church, and the final one of Pastor Fulton's ministry. The Bishop himself was present, having placed additional bread and wine upon the altar, but Pastor Fulton was too excited to notice this.

To his amazement, only a few feet in front of the altar stood the manger he had made so many years ago with his own hands; and lying in it was a tiny baby, moving its arms and legs and making all the sounds for which little ones are so much loved. About this Holy Family, however, there was something different. Mary was standing at the manger, and Joseph was sitting; and on the floor at his side lay a pair of crutches.

Under the leadership of Pastor Fulton, the music and scripture of the Nativity blended with the time-honored liturgy of the Sacrament. When it was time for the sermon, instead of going to the pulpit, Pastor Fulton went over to the manger and stood just back of Mary and Joseph where he could see the Baby Jesus. Then looking out toward this incredible congregation, he said, "First of all, I want to thank all of you for coming to this service. I don't know how your coming was arranged, but I can never thank you enough, and especially those who asked you to come. Second, as I bring my ministry to a close, I shall always remember with joy beyond words that you have come, and that at long last I have had once more a Holy Family at the Christmas Eve Service. And third, I do not know these wonderful people who are Mary and Joseph, and the Baby Jesus. I do not know how they came to be here, but I cannot escape the conviction that somehow the hand of God is present in this!"

At this point, though totally out of character, Joseph turned toward the old pastor, and said, "Pastor Fulton, I know this is very unusual, but may I say just a few words?"

"Please do," replied the pastor.

"Very well," continued the young man. "I hold here in my hand my Baptismal Certificate signed by Pastor George M. Fulton on August 1, 1948; and I am the son of Joe and Marian Neubel, members of Trinity Church until they were moved to the West Coast almost thirty years ago. And this," pointing to Mary, "is my wife, Jennie; and the Baby Jesus is our baby boy of three months, George Fulton Neubel.

"My beloved parents were married by Pastor Fulton at this very altar; and when I was born here at Brudersburg, the doctors told them that I might not live through the night. I was put into a special care unit, and Pastor Fulton was called to the hospital to baptize me. The doctors said that even if I were to live, I would probably be handicapped both physically and mentally. As you can see, I am handicapped physically, and without these crutches I would have to move about in a wheelchair. However, I am otherwise in excellent health; and thanks to God, and to my wonderful parents who still live in health and happiness on the West Coast, I was able to graduate from the University and the Conservatory of Music. My family and I have come back to Brudersburg because I have accepted a position as first violinist with the Brudersburg Symphony, beginning the middle of January. Before Pastor Fulton goes to his new home in the south, Jennie and I want him to baptize our infant son, his namesake."

With that, the young man resumed his role as Joseph, and no one could ever recall a Holy Family so reverent and beautiful.

Very quietly the Bishop came to the front of the church, and without saying a word, assisted the pastor with the bread and wine.

Finally, before sending the people forth with the Peace of Christ, Pastor Fulton and the good Bishop knelt in silent prayer at the altar. While they knelt there each of them felt a hand laid gently upon his shoulder. Concluding their prayer, they looked up, and there stood the young musician. His hands were trembling. Tears were streaming from his eyes. Through his tears a great light was shining. But his crutches were lying on the floor beside the manger!

Bethlehem

Long was the road to Bethlehem,
Where Joseph and his Mary came.
They are travel-worn, the day grows late,
As they reach the town with its towered gate—
The city of David's royal line—
And the stars of eve are beginning to shine.
They must seek a place where the poor may rest,
For Mary is weary and overpressed.
    . . . And it is the sixth hour.

They come to an inn and knock on the door,
Asking a little space, no more
Than a humble shelter in their need.
The innkeeper gives them scanty heed.
Little for strangers does he care—
His house is full. They must seek elsewhere.
Fearing to find no place that day,
Heavy at heart they turn away.
    . . . And it is the seventh hour.

In weariness and sore perplexed,
To a larger house they venture next.
Joseph for pity's sake begs again
A lodging for Mary in her pain.
They are poor Galileans, plain to be told—
Their garments are worn, their sandals are old.
The fat innkeeper jingles his keys,
And refuses shelter to such as these.
    . . . And it is the ninth hour.

Where now they turn the woman is kind,
The place is crowded, still she would find
Room for them somehow—moved at the sight
Of this gentle girl in her urgent plight,
Who tells of her hope and her strength far spent,
And seems to her woman's heart God-sent,
But the surly landlord roars in wrath
And sends them forth on their lonely path.
    . . . And it is the eleventh hour.

Still seeking a place to lay them down,
They come at length, on the edge of the town.
To a cattle-shed with sagging door,
Thankful for only the stable floor,
When an old gray donkey crowds to the wall
To make them room in his straw-laid stall.
And the cattle low at the stifled wail
Of a woman's voice in sore travail.
    . . . It is midnight and Mary's hour.

Over the place a great new star
Sheds wonder and glory beheld afar,
While all through the height of heaven there flies
The word of a seraph voice that cries,
"Glory to God, this wondrous morn
On earth the Saviour Christ is born."

BLISS CARMAN

The Christmas Story

Luke 2:1–20

For unto us a child is born, unto us a son is given: and the government shall be upon his shoulder: and his name shall be called Wonderful, Counsellor, The mighty God, The everlasting Father, The Prince of Peace.—ISAIAH 9:6

And it came to pass in those days, that there went out a decree from Caesar Augustus, that all the world should be taxed. (And this taxing was first made when Cyrenius was governor of Syria.) And all went to be taxed, every one into his own city. And Joseph also went up from Galilee, out of the city of Nazareth, into Judaea, unto the city of David, which is called Bethlehem; (because he was of the house and lineage of David:) To be taxed with Mary his espoused wife, being great with child.

And so it was, that, while they were there, the days were accomplished that she should be delivered. And she brought forth her firstborn son, and wrapped him in swaddling clothes, and laid him in a manger; because there was no room for them in the inn.

And there were in the same country shepherds abiding in the field, keeping watch over their flock by night. And, lo, the angel of the Lord came upon them, and the glory of the Lord shone round about them: and they were sore afraid.

And the angel said unto them, Fear not: for, behold, I bring you good tidings of great joy, which shall be to all people. For unto you is born this day in the city of David a Saviour, which is Christ the Lord. And this shall be a sign unto you; Ye shall find the babe wrapped in swaddling clothes, lying in a manger. And suddenly there was with the angel a multitude of the heavenly host praising God, and saying, Glory to God in the highest, and on earth peace, good will toward men. And it came to pass, as the angels were gone away from them into heaven, the shepherds said one to another, Let us now go even unto Bethlehem, and see this thing which is come to pass, which the Lord hath made known unto us.

And they came with haste, and found Mary, and Joseph, and the babe lying in a manger. And when they had seen it, they made known abroad the saying which was told them concerning this child. And all they that heard it wondered at those things which were told them by the shepherds. But Mary kept all these things, and pondered them in her heart. And the shepherds returned, glorifying and praising God for all the things that they had heard and seen, as it was told unto them.

Title

Author